The Quest to Safeguard Wholesome Family Life

other books by

Geshe Dakpa Topgyal

Death A Natural Part of Life

Diamond Key for Opening the Wisdom Eye

Essential Ethics

Holistic Health: A Tibetan Monk's View

Refuge

The Tibetan Buddhist Home Altar

Two Subtle Realities: Impermanence and Emptiness

Your Mind, Your Universe

Zuflucht — Buddhistische Zufluchtnahme

The Quest to Safeguard Wholesome Family Life

**CHILDREN'S EDUCATION, DISCIPLINE,
SUCCESS, AND SELF-LEADERSHIP
IN THE 21ST CENTURY**

Geshe Dakpa Topgyal

with Pamela Harrod

Radiant Mind Press
CHARLESTON, SOUTH CAROLINA

First Printing, 2020

ISBN 978-1-952518-00-3

Published by Radiant Mind Press
12 Parkwood Avenue
Charleston, South Carolina 29403
geshetopgyalbooks@gmail.com

Acknowledgements

THIS BOOK WOULD NOT have been possible without the kind and generous support from three of my virtuous friends. I must take the opportunity to thank all of them deeply and humbly. There is no better option to repay their kindness and support to bring this book to reality.

I start by humbly thanking Ms. Pamela Harrod, who collaborated with me for over two years on this endeavor. She sacrificed much time and energy to make this book what it is; a readable and helpful book for everyone to peruse and use as an aid to family life. From the beginning, she cleaned up my messy writing by checking and revising the work. In addition, she researched certain topics for the book to give readers important information on various subject matters.

With great respect, I want to thank Ms. Cynthia Laurrell for her great efforts in proof-reading the entire manuscript and diligently formatting the book to prepare it for publication.

I also wish to kindly thank Mr. Tsering Rabgyal, talented artist who trained at the Norbulingka Art Institute in Dharamsala, India. He designed and created the beautiful and meaningful artwork for the book cover.

Finally, I hope and pray that this book can help people gain a better and broader understanding of the importance of caring for children in a thoughtful and gentle manner. Learning beneficial skills and tools for raising children can certainly lead to a happier and more educated society.

I believe that a happy family is essential for attaining a happy and peaceful society. Without individual happy families, which are the smallest unit of society, happiness and peacefulness cannot spread to the entire society.

Geshe Dakpa Topgyal

Dedication

May there be happy couples,
Strongly bound with unconditional love.
May their love never decrease like a waning moon,
But increase like a waxing moon.

May happy couples have happy children,
May happy children have happy parents.
May happy parents and happy children,
Enjoy ample resources.

May every family find joy and happiness,
May all families have their needs met.
May all families have access to their endeavors,
May no family lack material resources to live comfortably.

May every child in society,
Have an equal opportunity for education.
May the education be guided by a sense of morality,
May the education be used to build a happy and able society.

May society have harmony.
May harmony bring joy and peace.
May joy and peace be a crop of society,
May the crop of peace dispel fear and conflict.

May racism and the cast system,
In societies be ceased.
May equanimity prevail,
From home to the entire world.

May there be happy families,
May there be peaceful societies.
May there be a sense of sisterhood and brotherhood.
May there be oneness of humankind.

May there be no war.
May there be no famine.
May there be no epidemic diseases.
May there be no other known or unknown calamities.

Contents

Authors' Introduction

MANY OF US SHARE hopes of having a close-knit family, with members staying in intimate contact and harmony for the duration of their lifetimes. Although this may be the desire of many, too often in this modern world it may not be the case as, unlike in the past, we live in a more troubled time.

In order to make our aspirations more attainable, we should try to concentrate on the quality of our life and our relationships with family members and others. By focusing our minds on goodness, love, compassion, and forgiveness, we can develop a deeper understanding and holistic view of our intimate connection with people and nature. An emotional hygiene of trust, loyalty, respect, and sympathy can be cultivated and grow into living a life of contentment and moderation. We can thus develop a sense of concern for others' well-being more than for ourselves.

But what about the help and guidance we need with the struggles we all face in our daily lives? At some point, everyone will have to confront family concerns, problems with our jobs, illnesses, financial matters, and the death of loved ones. While some of these situations may be commonplace and expected, others may arise without warning and with little understanding of how we should deal with these problems or concerns.

Certainly, taking care of oneself, being in good physical health, having adequate material resources, strong emotional and mental balance, moral and ethical qualities, and educational qualifications are all very valuable foundations for finding the answers. However, can these qualities be sufficient to provide us with the means to comprehensively analyze the symptoms and possible solutions to our problems? Where should we turn to find the skills needed to truly understand and deal with our problems?

In our present-day technological and materialistic world, there are mounting negative conditions in society which we often do not address openly or correctly. Although we are not direct products of social conditions, we can be deeply affected by them. This can cause confusion and uncertainty in our thinking. Therefore, we need to learn how can we live in society in a meaningful way, and yet not be overly influenced by all of the things society throws at us.

One solution to consider for solving our problems is found in an ancient philosophy of life. It is a philosophy that is perfectly relevant in our modern world, from simple family life to the global level. How can this be so? Our mind is often very confused and misunderstands what we see, what we think, what we feel, and what we want. This ancient philosophy can help us to better understand our problems and learn how to cope with them more wisely.

CHAPTER 1

Social Conditions that Affect Individuals' Lives

I N OUR MODERN WORLD, we often lack knowledge and awareness of social ethics. If used mindfully, these skills can contribute to constructive and responsible actions and behaviors that help create more harmony and less conflict in our world. We seem to be bombarded with opinions of how to think, act, and dress, what to believe in, what is moral, who to vote for, and what is right and what is wrong. Instead of being taught important life skills and lessons by our parents and families, we are often being shaped by society, including government, social media, news outlets, advertisements, politicians, activists, books, television, and films. This "artificial life" that we commonly believe is genuine and worthy of heeding advice from can lead to wrong thinking and wrong actions. These influences can subtlety yet strongly control our thoughts and actions, robbing us of our rights and freedoms as individuals.

In our present-day materialistic society, we face a growing number of personal problems and difficulties, partly owing to widespread negative social conditions, such as drug abuse, alcoholism, domestic violence, and family breakdowns. Every day on television, in newspapers, and other media outlets we are exposed in vivid detail to war, killings, abductions, abuse, kidnappings, suicides, adultery, and bitter divorces. Our minds store these images of negative social conditions and as a consequence, we live with disturbed minds that may trigger negative thoughts, emotions, and actions. This is how negative social conditions affect individuals' lives, which in turn can have negative impacts on society.

These detrimental social problems are growing year by year. It may be difficult for us to notice these changes, as they occur little by little. Therefore, we must pay close attention and address these changes in a clear and timely manner. Regrettably, as long as there is a steady and constant inflow of money and resources, we typically feel satisfied with our situation. Only when negative conditions begin to affect us do we become motivated to call for change and begin to see that these conditions are negative to ourselves, our families, and the society as a whole.

Negative social conditions grow like mold inside our homes. Just as mold is extremely bad for our health and well-being, negative social conditions are likewise bad for our health and well-being. We are social creatures and we must live together in society; we cannot isolate ourselves from others, just as we cannot quarantine ourselves inside our homes. The society in which we live needs to be a healthy, wholesome, and educated one, similar to our houses needing to be clean, well-organized, well insulated, and structurally sound. Our homes and our societies should have positive energy that allows us to be happy and well-functioning in our environment.

Influences contributing to these negative conditions may include the outcomes of materialism and consumerism, which strive to emphasize our wants and desires. More and more, we are convinced that in order to be happy and healthy, we need to nurture and pamper ourselves in gyms and spas, boost our self-esteem with fancy clothes and cars, cure boredom by eating at restaurants and meeting friends at bars, and never hesitating to act on a whim to buy anything that catches our attention.

People in modern societies are becoming robotic consumers, partly due to the stimuli of captivating advertisements as well as companies emphasizing profit over other considerations. These influences can make us lose control of our decision-making abilities and ultimately our lives. What we decide to purchase or not purchase is, to a certain degree, determined by social pressures and the commercial dominance of television, movies, and other media. We recurrently go into debt due to buying many needless things without thinking of the consequences. It is as if we are being forced to see only the artificial life of television and movies instead of the real life in our very homes and neighborhoods. Rather than living real lives, we are living unrealistic and unhealthy dream lives.

Nowadays, almost everything we do becomes a competition to win, be the best, have the most beautiful and intelligent children, and find success in every way possible. This creates enormous pressure on our lives. The sense of competition brings out feelings of anxiety, depression, aggression, suicidal thoughts, and loneliness. These highly damaging mental, emotional, and psychological problems are becoming more widespread in the societies in which we live.

Our communities have become unhealthy and difficult places to live a serene life and find the peace and stability required to raise our innocent children in a healthy way. With so much focus on material goods and our social status, our mental, ethical, and moral well-being are being sorely neglected. We are often told to believe that moral and ethical education belongs to religion and are not to be discussed or taught in schools or in society as a whole. Our "dream life" of TV, movies, books, and other media has a certain romanticism where we are led to believe in "me" — that my own concepts of ethics and morals are of utmost importance.

Just as important, many members of society feel isolated from the mainstream, leaving many people vulnerable and in need of various types of help. Racism, gender discrimination, unemployment or lack of stable employment, and economic inequalities are some of the many issues facing society. These influences are invading all groups, leading to dysfunctional thoughts and behaviors.

In our current state of affairs, there are fewer and fewer moral and ethical limits of what can or should be advertised on TV, the

Internet, or other forms of media. Similarly, there are less and less moral or legal boundaries on what can be said or what behaviors viewers should be exposed to. Most of the media is open to the public from age 1 to 100+, with little guidance or prohibitions. Is being allowed to say or do virtually "anything" in the media a good model and use of freedom in our society? Are boundaries always a negative concept that will make our society less free, with fewer human rights? Are we free when we cannot feel safe on the streets, in airplanes, or in school? Are we free when we feel afraid to express our thoughts and beliefs, especially if they differ from what current society dictates?

Our lives are being overwhelmed by the Internet, the media, big business, and advertisers. We are exposed to unwholesome movies, TV programs, and music lyrics. Without being aware, we hear propaganda or misleading and mind-luring concepts and ideas. We are becoming more and more disconnected from a genuine, wholesome society, which seems almost alien to us. The result is more suffering for humankind. Human society cannot afford to continue down this path. There is seldom a sunrise with people looking forward to a day with all good news, and rarely a sunset in which to look back on the day without bad news.

Do we candidly discuss these issues in open forums, with genuine sincerity to try and find solutions? Probably not at all. As long as we are not the victims, we are prone to ignore the problems. We also tend to normalize troubles that reoccur frequently, such as not aiding a stranger in need, driving dangerously, or much more seriously having shootings in schools. Only a decade or two ago, a shooting in a school was met with outrage and disbelief. Nowadays, this extreme form of violence in schools is hardly talked about, even when young students protest against such acts. For some, owning a gun is akin to a normal thing to have in the home, just as owning a TV is normal. This is how our societies are becoming increasingly negative, unhealthy, and unsafe places for every one of us, especially our children, to live, survive, and flourish.

A healthy society is extremely important to help insure the happiness of the populace. Understand that happiness does not mean a society filled with beautiful material goods and facilities. Rather, it means a peaceful, educated, well-mannered, co-existing, inclusive society, with a focus on each individual's positive development, including an emphasis on goodness and kindness. A healthy society should develop bonds of affection and coming together to help one another, rather than ignoring or exploiting each other. Our modern societies are not integrated, but more disintegrated with self-interest groups, large gaps between the rich and the poor, and discrimination.

With all of these problems, can we indeed call our societies "modern"? Shouldn't these problems be considered antiquated and shunned? A perfect society may be impossible to create and keep, but a society with as few negative conditions as possible is attainable. As long as societies are egocentric or passive, there cannot be a peaceful world.

We are all very much aware of many negative conditions in the societies in which we live. But human society is a group of individuals, and we are all members of that society. There may not be many immediate solutions available to solve these problems, but there is a real possibility that we can individually make positive changes within ourselves, making sure not to become victims of or trapped by these negative social conditions. There are many positive ways in which we can make changes within ourselves to help protect our children, our families, and our communities. In the following chapters, we will discuss and explain them in depth.

CHAPTER 2

The Relationship Between Husband and Wife

WHILE A WIFE AND HUSBAND are two separate, unique, and different persons, they should live together as one secure and protected embodiment of love. Spouses need to be married in their hearts and minds, and not just with a legal document for the public to view. Finding the right life-long partner is one of the most important and difficult decisions a person will make in their life. The couple needs to get to know each other very well before getting married, as it takes time to discern the inner qualities of the other person. Knowing, understanding, and accepting the values, interests, beliefs, and additional traits of the other person are necessary to help ensure that the marriage will last and lead to a happy and healthy family life. Getting married in a hasty way — love at first sight, as romantics would say — can certainly lead to a troubled and unhappy marriage. Consequently, it is very important to allow adequate time to become quite familiar with a potential spouse regarding his or her ways of thinking, habits, ethics, conduct, and mental and emotional stability. Most importantly, both parties should have serious discussions about the moral responsibilities of being a wife or a husband.

The genuine value of marriage is for both spouses to have a life-long working love partnership, where husband and wife unfailingly offer support and comfort to each other, especially in times of tragedy, illness, and misfortune. The nature of married life should be wholesome and nourishing, since this has a strong effect on all aspects of their children's lives. Troubled parents will likely result in having troubled children. Both husband and wife must understand that being a parent is not an easy undertaking, as both parents are the first and most important teachers for their children. Raising children requires parents to sacrifice much of their leisure time and independence to care for their needy offspring. This can also be stated in a more positive way by saying: *Caring for children empowers parents to dedicate as much of their free time as possible to the upbringing of their precious children.* The parents' primary roles are to give their children proper direction and guidance before sending them into the real world, which is not always as soft and fragrant as a rose.

Husband and wife relationships involve far more than living under one roof, sharing a bed, eating dinner at nice restaurants, and saying words such as honey or sweetie. There are several important and necessary aspects and responsibilities associated with successful wife-husband relationships. A wholesome and stable marriage requires both partners to be loyal, trustworthy, and willing to sacrifice fifty percent of their freedom for the sake of the other. They both need to be prepared to listen intensely, carefully, and sincerely to each other, be accepting of each other's opinions or ideas, and be willing to make plans or projects together based on mutual agreement. The spouses must be respectful of each other's needs and sensitivities. Husbands and wives ought to share in all household responsibilities such as cooking, cleaning, doing the dishes, laundry, grocery shopping, and yard work. Moms and dads should participate in their children's activities as well as taking them to appointments, school, lessons, and other obligations. In a traditional way, the couple should protect the well-being of their children, with the mother providing nourishment and the father being a protector. The parents and children need to spend joyful time together with a sense of family togetherness.

Family life can be very challenging and demanding. Relationships between husbands and wives are not easily maintained without having unconditional love, care, and devotion for each other. More often than not, there are ways to find solutions or coping mechanisms for many problems that may arise. Inflexibility and resistance can be subdued with flexibility and acceptance. It may require much effort, understanding, patience, and humility to deal with many marital problems. Otherwise, the lifeblood of the marriage may be defeated by obtaining a legal divorce. In many cases, divorce is actually a failure of the marriage rather than a solution for the couple's problems. Divorce is often not due to what happened, but rather how the couple responded to their issues. Correspondently, life's troubles are not always about problems and disputes, but how we choose to react to them.

No man is perfect. No woman is perfect. Consequently, there cannot be a perfect marriage free from any difficulties. Problems and conflicts will arise at some point in the life of every marriage. Disagreements may arise from the smallest and seemingly unimportant matters. If one or both spouses are not willing to share equally in the responsibilities of day-to-day living, this can indisputably lead to deep problems. For example, if a husband likes to have home-cooked meals, but seldom helps with the shopping, food preparation, or cleanup, his wife may react with negative emotions. Likewise, if he prepares a tasty dinner and his wife says that she doesn't like his cooking and walks away from the kitchen, he may feel apathetic. Often, one of the two ends up doing everything, which easily leads to negative emotions that can fester and grow. If this type of behavior continues and becomes the norm, one day his or her heart will cry out with tears of anger and frustration. This type of situation can result from not sharing or caring about the joint familial responsibilities of husband and wife. If there is a lack of mutual understanding and concern for the importance of why they need to divide household duties, mutual happiness and closeness will suffer. With understanding, caring, and appreciation of the importance of sharing household responsibilities, a couple's love commitment to each other will flourish and grow.

The following qualities illustrate how being negligent in a marriage can lead to serious problems, some of which may be very difficult to overcome. In order for couples to maintain a successful marriage, with the prosperity of love, honesty, and compassion, both spouses should joyfully embrace and cultivate certain important qualities. Developing these traits will take hard work, diligence, concern for the spouse, and a humble heart. These qualities include:

Be Faithful

What is the meaning of faithfulness, especially in regard to marriage? Does it simply mean not cheating on your spouse? Fortunately, it means much more than that. Faithfulness involves actions, thoughts, and behaviors whereby a person can comfortably and fully trust in another person without any room for suspicion. It is being consistently loyal, devoted, and truthful in all aspects of the relationship. For followers of certain religions, being truthful and loyal in one's relationship with God is being faithful. In this context, faithfulness is a quality of the relationship with one's spouse — the relationship of husband and wife. This quality will actually strengthen and deepen if and when the relationship is built and continues to grow with trust, honesty, and security. Faithfulness must be cultivated and nurtured in order for the relationship to maintain a sense of abiding and enduring freshness.

Be Loyal

Being loyal in marriage is demonstrating unwavering support and devotion for the spouse, so that he or she can peacefully trust in their partner's allegiance without any fear or reservations. Loyalty is always being at his or her side when needed, with a willingness to look after their well-being with no thought or intent of betrayal or deception. Loyalty is one of the most important ingredients in rela-

10

tionships, particularly those between husband and wife, parents and children, and clerics and disciples. These types of relationships are formed with deep-rooted elements of loyalty, love, respect, devotion, trust, and a natural purity. These components work as a "glue" to hold the relationship together with a strong and stable bond, leaving no room to be lost or damaged by internal or external forces.

The marital relationship between a wife and husband is sacrosanct and is meant to last a lifetime. Breaking the marital relationship by betrayal, adultery, disrespect, dishonesty, or withdrawing love from the spouse by abandoning him or her for selfish interests is without question a grave transgression. Disregarding the law of corresponding effects due to interactions with others through mutual feelings of attraction is a serious wrongdoing. Causing pain and suffering in the heart of the spouse, family, or friend by any misdeed is also a grave failing. Ironically, these actions can also bring delight to one's enemies. The loss of loyalty caused by these types of behaviors is one of the worst things you can do, and the outcomes can cause severe emotional, physical, and monetary hardship for your spouse, children, or friend.

It is easy to see that many dogs are unfailingly loyal to their owners and can become very stressed in their absence. Dogs exhibit many acts of loyalty towards their master; they respect, obey, and listen attentively to them. They often can be found sitting outside the door, instinctively protecting their human keeper. Even with separations for long periods of time, the loyalty seldom lessens. Dogs do not seek a new master by looking for a better partner. If a master dies, a dog will truly grieve, and may even spend time sitting at his or her grave. The dog's devotion is unending.

Loyalty among humans can and should be a natural way to act, especially towards loved ones. Dogs do not need a legal ceremony in order to be faithful. The relationship between husbands and wives should demonstrate the innate relationship between married couples. Loyalty is an extremely important part of a relationship, without which the marital bond can become fragile — without durability, like a snowflake in the sun. Most importantly, loyalty needs to be cultivated, respected, and protected by both spouses. Without this devotion, the relationship cannot last a lifetime with a genuine value for each other.

Be Respectful

It is essential for both spouses to be humble, gentle, and polite towards one another by appreciating the other as wholly worthy of their trust. Both individuals need to be very mindful to consistently be kind, loving, caring, and putting the needs of the spouse ahead of one's own personal wants or needs. In general, being respectful means holding someone to a high regard in your life and wholeheartedly following in his or her steps with a deep sense of admiration. To be respectful to your spouse certainly does not mean to bow down or throw yourself before your spouse's feet. Rather, it means perceiving him or her as an everlasting beautiful flower in your heart, to cherish with unconditional love, caring, and loyalty.

Be Tolerant

Tolerance is being open-minded, with a willingness to listen calmly to other's thoughts, beliefs, or perspectives that may not be in concordance with one's own. Tolerance does not mean having to accept or approve of these beliefs, but rather to be able to have a clear mind, ready to listen and deal with circumstances as they arise without unnecessary discord. Moreover, tolerance is a powerful faculty of the mind to accept another's aggression or wrongdoing without becoming angry, upset, or placing blame without contemplating the possibility that you may also be showing aggression or have contributed to the wrongdoing of the other.

In the case of a wife and husband, tolerance may mean accepting the other's wrongdoing without causing severe or irreversible damage to the marital relationship. Husbands and wives really need to understand that no woman is perfect, and no man is perfect. Both spouses may, from time to time, make minor mistakes or errors in judgment. The important thing to remember is that tolerance is necessary in these circumstances to avoid worsening the situation. We must allow room for mistakes, errors, or even angry outbursts. Tolerance and acceptance are very important for marital relationships to be strong and lasting.

> *Please note that accepting or understanding minor mistakes, errors, or aggression does not mean that anyone should accept or tolerate abuse or continual aggressive behavior.*

Be Less Defensive

We humans are very prone to personalize things, especially issues that we disagree with or find offensive. When we take things too personally or too seriously, we often mentally hammer the issue until it pierces into our hearts. When we personalize how our spouse treats us at certain times, we may experience all sorts of negative emotions, such as anger, worry, jealousy, and suspicion. Our perceptions of the events may become very painful and more serious than they truly are. We can become defensive and feel offended at the same time. There is then no room for being tolerant, as our perceptions are not based on a true understanding of the situation.

There are times when your spouse may undeniably say or do things that are not very pleasant or kind. You, in turn, may want to hit back with a verbal arrow to hurt him or her. Most of the time when these occurrences happen, we do not stop to think if he or she really meant to hurt or insult us. To help prevent this from happening, instead of being defensive, we need to try to be more compatible. Try to think of something your spouse may have said or done that was pleasant and appealing to you. Use these thoughts as an echo, which you can use to bounce the negative, ego-driven defensiveness away. This positive action can help maintain a healthy relationship with your spouse without being wounded by your own negative reactions to your spouse's unpleasantness. Never allow yourself to be hit by a negative arrow from your spouse. Remember — staying together in times of happiness and unhappiness or fortune and misfortune should be the most important part of your marriage commitment.

Be Willing to Sacrifice Fifty Percent of Your Personal Time for the Sake of Your Spouse

Getting married to someone you love, but not being willing to devote at least half of your free time for his or her sake will not be conducive to a happy, fulfilling married life. Marriage means being united, with a desire to be with your spouse. Wanting to be independent and unwilling to spend a good portion of your time with your spouse, sharing thoughts, plans, and interests will defeat the whole purpose of getting married. A desire for independence or exclusiveness rather than inclusiveness from one or both partners will not lead to a long-lasting marriage. In such situations, it cannot be possible to find any true meaning or purpose to the marriage. The marriage will become like the dry season, where plants wither without precious rainfall. As with the lack of rainfall leading to wilting plants, the marriage will wither and wilt away without a strong sense of sharing and togetherness. You will feel alone, like the one plant that is barely surviving in the parched earth.

Truthfully and practically, both spouses lose about fifty percent of their freedom on the day they marry. Since this is part of the reality of marriage, one should knowingly live in concordance with this actuality. This is the only way to ensure that the marriage will be long lasting and will not be a lonely, unfulfilling union. A collaborative marriage will bear much more meaning and serve a good purpose for the family you and your spouse create. No one will need to feel like a lonely plant in the dry season.

Be Sensitive

Being sensitive means much more than being a kind and caring person towards others. Having sensitivity is more like a skill, a "radar", or an internal ability or awareness to be able to "read" another person's feelings, thoughts, or emotions. It is taking notice of something about the other person, whether it is a new dress, haircut, or looking tired, worried, or joyful about something. Sensitivity is about being unselfish, genuine, and putting another person's cares and concerns above your own.

In marriage, the more sensitive each spouse is towards the other, the deeper the understanding, bond, and love will be. Both spouses need to be sensitive to the other's feelings, moods, beliefs, fragility of emotions, and his or her needs. A need may be as simple as a loving hug, or much more serious wants. Being sensitive means to know how to avoid saying or doing things that annoy or bother your spouse, along with a willingness to say or do the things that are more agreeable to him or her. One of the most important things to remember is to make sure that your spouse's needs are met in a timely manner. This does not mean that your spouse should make demands or deadlines. It is simply a sign of respect, caring, and love on your part to make sure to fulfill the needs of your husband or wife. When you go to work, you know what priorities need to be accomplished first. The same can be said for a husband and wife relationship. When you awaken in the morning, take notice of your spouse with a kind greeting and the sensitivity to see if your spouse seems to be feeling well. Being unresponsive to your spouse, especially at the start of the day, can lead to many problems in your relationship. Over time, negligence toward your spouse can result in him or her having negative emotions and feeling fragile, insecure, unloved, and fearful. Blame, criticism, disrespect, disregard, and alienation can then emerge in the relationship.

Being sensitive is an important quality for maintaining a meaningful husband and wife relationship. It shows your spouse that you care. *Zha-Tsang* is a Tibetan phrase meaning "love bond partnership" — the way to lead a domestic life together. A love bond partnership between a wife and husband is all about togetherness — to live together, eat together, hold hands together, stand together in happy and unhappy times, work together, raise children together, and share success and failure together. It also means moving along the rough road of aging together to provide help and comfort to each other until the time comes to die. A love bond marriage will not die while the wife and husband are married in their hearts. It can only die at the time of physical death.

~ ~ ~ ~ ~

In today's world many people do not get married in their hearts, with a serious commitment to sustain the union for a lifetime. Instead, people often marry for romance, a cure for loneliness, financial support, or the desire to have a spouse to make them happy by giving and doing things that they desire. This lack of serious commitment is one of the primary problems with married life in the modern world. A casual appreciation of marriage is one important reason why the divorce rate is so high, especially in more developed countries. To help counter this trend, young people should not rush into marriage; rather, they should first establish their own adult identity by completing their education, finding a good job, and becoming somewhat secure financially. In addition, young people need to be mature enough to understand the true meaning of marriage, the responsibilities it entails, and the life-long moral and love commitments needed to maintain a healthy, worthy, and enduring marriage. Doing so should help couples avoid many problems that may arise during the course of married life.

In contemporary cultures, the intended outcome of dating is often to find a suitable spouse. Once this is achieved, the twosome has achieved their goal — often beginning with a big, fancy wedding and a glamorous honeymoon. There may be little thought of other factors of their union, such as fitting in with each other's family, culture, religious views, compatibility, economic expectations, and how to raise children. The concept of "true love will conquer all because I married the person I love" is ingrained in many of today's societies. In other words, if I fall in love, that in itself should guarantee a happy marriage.

Many, if not most people in modern societies firmly believe in having the freedom to fall in love and marry whomever they chose, even with the disapproval of their parents. The thought of accepting advice or guidance in finding a partner for life is anathema to many young people. They may feel that it is none of their parents' business to approve of whom they are planning to wed. They may ask themselves, "How could I possibly find life-long happiness with a person I was forced to marry?"

In some areas of the world, particularly in parts of Asia, the Middle East, South America, and Africa, the family has traditionally played a key role in finding a suitable marriage partner for their son or daughter. These so-called "arranged marriages" are often believed to be solely orchestrated by the parents, with no consent needed from the children. Generally, children are a part of the decision-making process, with an understanding that finding an appropriate spouse is a family responsibility. One of the main priorities is to ensure that the partner forms a close and secure relationship with the entire family, not simply a husband and wife union.

The concept of genuine love between a couple is largely misunderstood in the Western world and other modern-day cultures. The modern view of love mainly focuses on romantic love; the type of love we are exposed to by watching films, reading romance novels, listening to rock and country music lyrics, and perhaps by witnessing a royal wedding on TV. These influences have helped to condition the minds of virtually everyone in society, and especially the youth, who seek to independently find their true love by their own devices, very often without any help or influence from their parents. Falling in love with the first person dated or a good-looking stranger, perhaps from an "exotic" culture, can indeed be very persuasive.

Along with this, many marriages seem to be based on financial or self-centered interests, with little concern for long-term marriage stability. Quite a few people get married with a preconceived mental strategy to divorce if things do not go as well as planned. Couples often do not look for or care about the inner qualities of the person they are planning to marry. They tend to be more interested in superficial things or social partialities, such as what political party they are in allegiance with, the type of job he or she has, how much money they earn, and how they spend their leisure time.

A person who marries someone that simply meets their preferred criteria may often lead to a failed marriage that ends in a difficult divorce. Why is this so? Because, while agreeing on social and political matters, having a good job, and enjoying the same activities are not bad, they have very little to do with the genuine inner qualities of the other person. Virtues such as kindness, humility, trust, and fairness are far more important than the superficial characteristics of the person. The authentic virtues and true beauty of a person lie within his or her heart, not on his or her skin. A Tibetan saying that relates to this concept is: "The beauty of a man or a woman is to be found within him or her. But the beauty of a tiger is surely to be found on its skin." This is why people may choose to wear a fur coat as an ornament of clothing. Therefore, it is wise to marry a person with an inner beauty that you can love and cherish, rather than his or her external, superficial features. Before getting married, a man should make sure that he has room in his heart to trust his future wife. He must also make sure that he is worthy of her trust. Likewise, a woman should make sure that she has room in her heart for her future husband's trust, and that she is worthy of his trust. Both the man and woman should give sincere pledges of each other's conviction through their actions, and not just with words that may slip over the tongue.

Once married, both spouses should avoid having unreasonable doubts, suspicions, or jealous feelings or surveilling the other, thinking that the spouse may be doing something outside of the marital relationship. These suspicions can only create many unnecessary and baseless problems in the marriage. The ordinary mind or perception is capable of creating something and then projecting those thoughts onto things or objects. Whatever the mind projects onto the thing or object can reflect back to one's own perception as being real on an objective level. In the case of a spouse, he or she may not have done anything wrong outside of the marital relationship, but the mind of the suspicious spouse may project their thoughts onto the other spouse based on an invalid interpretation. The suspicious spouse may be convinced that their thoughts are genuinely true, although it is utterly baseless and not true at all. If either spouse has these types of thoughts, they can be very devastating to the marriage. Needless to say, every spouse should have the right to address the other's wrongdoings if there is solid evidence that should not be dismissed or ignored.

Because many people marry without a deep sense of commitment and devotion in their hearts, couples may become more focused on social activities, romance, and having fun. Over time, the marriage may melt away when the fun goes away. In former generations, people often married out of heart-felt devotion or a sense of commitment towards the spouse, knowing that their marriage would not end until one spouse passed away. In the past, the majority of married people did not remarry after their spouse died. One reason for this was that they knew that their marriage was a dual lifetime commitment, and not something that could be replaced with another spouse. The spouse's body may have been buried in a graveyard, but the true person was buried in the spouse's heart. The spouse who survived did not need to remarry since his or her heart was full and comfortable. Instead of remarrying, he or she would use their time, energy, and attention to take care of their children and keep the family bonds strong and lasting. The surviving spouse would try his or her best to provide the children with a good education and moral guidance, knowing that the deceased spouse would want the children to be looked after first and foremost.

This example demonstrates how one's moral love duty can be fulfilled on behalf of the spouse after he or she passes away. One should try not to feel overly lonely after the death of the spouse. Being fully aware of the emotional necessity to stave off loneliness can help prevent the need to look for another partner. Immediately searching for a stranger to cure loneliness is not a good remedy for becoming a widow or widower. It is certainly not wrong to remarry, but it is important to make certain that all of the necessary matters needed to fulfill the deceased spouse's hopes and wishes are taken care of. It is also important to allow oneself time to rest, reflect, and live in peace for a length of time. This is plainly the best way to resolve the passing of one's life partner.

In brief, marriage should last a lifetime. Genuine love is the true wealth of marriage. Trust and loyalty are the life force of marriage.

Doing things side by side, spending quiet time together, and making sure that your spouse's needs are met are what will help keep the marriage strong. Make sure not to bring the workplace problems home to bother your spouse with unnecessary worries. Be mindful to be on time whenever your spouse needs you and your help. Raise your children in partnership with love and affection from both parents. Do not be stubborn in your thinking or rigid in your thoughts or actions. Be flexible, open minded, and speak soft words to each other. Lay gentle hands on your children. Be kind and tender in your private life and strong and unified in public life. In doing so, your married life will be happy and the purpose of living together as a husband and wife will be fulfilled with joy and happiness. Lastly, both spouses must have equal rights and responsibilities in making all decisions concerning the marriage and the family.

~ ~ ~ ~ ~

Sadly, divorce is becoming more and more prevalent around the world. More often than not, divorce is not a solution for a problematic marriage. It is more an ultimate failure of the marriage itself. That being said, divorce is acceptable or necessary in certain circumstances. When conditions in the marriage involve adultery, abuse (both physical or psychological), domestic violence, alcoholism, drug addiction, gambling, or serious moral or ethical problems, the victim of any of these ordeals needs to seek help and guidance to decide the best course of action to take. A divorce can be imperative for the sake of the family's well-being, especially if children are involved. Other than these types of situations, divorcing for self-serving interests is negative and not acceptable on moral grounds.

Parents considering separation or divorce need to be aware of the impact divorce or troubled marriages can have on innocent children. Academic difficulties, increased drug and alcohol use and abuse, and psychological distress are much more common among children and teens exposed to these situations. Divorced parents, commonly the mother, often face severe financial difficulties due to reduced income. The primary caregiver (typically the mother) may need to juggle a heavier workload at home and in the workplace. This in turn, leaves less time to care for the children. Living arrangements for children of divorce or separation are often divided between the parents, with little understanding of how this may affect the children. Just imagine how unsettling and rootless it would feel to spend a few days at one place, and another few days at another place. It would be akin to the life of a traveling salesperson, constantly living out of a suitcase. For a child, it could cause dire consequences. They may feel like a guest or virtual stranger in one or both homes, totally left out of family life. Adding to the stress would be stepbrothers or stepsisters. This could lead to being confused about who their parents and siblings really are, fearful of not being loved, and feeling partially abandoned by one or both parents.

We can see that innocent children of separated or divorced parents often pay a heavy toll, as their protective home environment has been torn apart. Choosing to divorce for selfish reasons is an extremely negative action to take when children are involved, including teenage children. Unless the reasons for divorce or separation are truly valid, it is in the best interest of the children to stay married and work on getting along for their sake. It is the moral thing to do. Needless selfish divorce simply punishes the innocent child's life. It really cuts the child's life into two, with no easy way to mend the wounds and sew the child's life back into one.

Please note: This is not to say that divorce itself is negative in a religious sense. However, divorce always has a negative impact on the healthy upbringing of children and their future lives.

Staying single is much better than getting married in the first place and then divorcing after a few years. You may spend ten thousand dollars on your wedding day and then spend forty thousand dollars on divorce proceedings, all the while undergoing legal battles and heartache. Love, romance, dreams, and excitement in intergender relationships are fine before you find the person you decide to marry. However, when it comes time to get married, you should think very carefully and deeply about the decision you are about to make, while leaving romance, dreams, and excitement behind. At this time, you need to make the decision to give away fifty percent of your freedom and leisure time for your spouse's sake.

CHAPTER 3

The Natural Relationship Between Parents and Children

T HERE IS A NATURAL relationship bond between parents and their children that begins at the time of conception. The connection between parent and child may also be linked to causal outcomes established by actions in previous lives. By definition, the term "parents" means a male and a female together contributing a part of each of their genes for the basis of forming the biological body of their offspring in the female's womb. In the conventional world, the male contributor is named father and the female contributor is named mother. The male contributes sperm, in a similar way to fertilizer, and the female contributes an egg, which is the actual potential seed for the formation of the biological body of the fetus. From the moment of conception, the father's role is primarily to provide protection and the mother's role is to provide nourishment to the offspring. The natural relationship between parents and their children originates from the contributed biological elements of the parents that serve as a basis for the formation of the biological body of the offspring. This natural relationship is the sole source for the parents' moral responsibility to look after their offspring's well-being. It is also the offspring's moral duty to fulfill the hopes and wishes of their parents with unconditional respect, honor, obedience, and humility.

It is very important to recognize and understand the seriousness of this concept, as it is the unequalled basis for family order and well-being. Sometimes, people who are expecting a child may have wrong feelings or misunderstandings about this situation. Some may be excited, seeing a baby as cute and someone to show off to the world. Others may want a child because their siblings and friends have children. Some may not want a child at all, with the pregnancy being an "accident".

This natural relationship is partially bound by attachment and love. Since attachment is part of the connection, separation between the parents and their children will by nature be painful on both sides. Because love is also a part of the relationship, a deep wish to be happy will naturally be strong on the both sides, parents and children, and should last for an entire lifetime. This connection is innately pure, sacred, and essential for the child's survival and healthy growth, both physically and mentally. Without parents' proper care and love, a child has no means to survive and the child may likely die. Therefore, there is no substitute for the kindness of parents and the genuine love for their children. In actuality, we are all still children and have survived solely because of the kindness of our parents, whether they are still living or deceased.

In good situations, parents and children follow these precepts instinctively. Sadly, there are quite a few instances where parents do abandon their children, either physically or emotionally. Likewise, children (and also grown children) may forget their parents' kindness, not take care of parents in need, or show a lack of respect towards their parents. In all of these cases, these actions should be considered as grave "sins". There is no greater misbehavior than these types of conduct. Parents cannot genuinely feel happy in their parental roles, and children cannot be truly happy children under these circumstances. It is very likely that they will not be able to succeed in their worldly endeavors owing to the grave "sins" of abandonment and being forgotten.

Love and attachment bonds are the core of universal natural relationships between all parents and their offspring for all forms of life, regardless of the type of pregnancy (birth from womb or from hatching an egg). We may think that there could not be a natural relationship between a mother turtle and her babies, since there is no contact between the two after she lays her eggs in the sand near the ocean or in the mud. Once the mother turtle lays her eggs, she returns to her home — in the ocean or on land — and never meets with her offspring again. It seems as though the mother turtle truly abandons her eggs and has no instinct to look after the eggs after they hatch. However, this is not the case. The natural relationship between a mother turtle and her offspring begins several weeks before laying her clutch of eggs. Nearing the end of gestation, female turtles search for a safe place to lay their eggs. In this way of bonding with her offspring, the mother is trying to ensure that the eggs will be hatched and able to survive. Once the eggs are laid, she will typically cover the eggs with sand or mud so that they can stay warm and safe until they hatch. At this time, her physical role of protecting and caring for her offspring is complete. However, she has not truly abandoned her eggs, as she has prepared them for a safe birth.

To explain this natural relationship in more detail, the reason why the mother turtle's eggs will hatch is because of her memory of laying the eggs and her thoughts that the eggs will hatch. Therefore, the mother turtle's memory about laying the eggs and her thoughts that the eggs will hatch serves as a basis for the natural relationship between the mother turtle and her hatchlings. The need for nourishment also comes from the mother turtle's memory and her understanding that her eggs will hatch after some time. Turtles' eggs cannot hatch and survive without the mother's care and nourishment through affectionate thoughts, which also come from her memory. This natural relationship exists between the mother turtle and her baby turtles, even though they have never physically met after the eggs were laid in the sand or mud. Therefore, the naturally imprinted memory of the mother allows for the eggs to be kept safe from harm and for the offspring to receive nourishment. In all of nature, this natural relationship is an indispensable condition for the survival of the offspring, based on the parent's tireless moral responsibility to look after the well-being of their brood.

In humans, these conditions are necessary to ensure the offspring's development of proper growth to maturity with sound mental and physical health. Parents' unconditional love for their children and the children's unconditional respect and dutiful behavior toward their parents are the most important parts of the natural relationship. The parent-child relationship certainly will become strong and healthy if these conditions are wholeheartedly established in the hearts and minds of both parents and their children. This will truly bring happiness to the entire family — both parents and children. In some ways, this should not be necessary to even mention, as we can certainly see this loving relationship among many families within our societies.

It is extremely important for our collective societies to place a higher value on understanding the importance of the relationship between parents and children. We should cherish this relationship and make certain to maintain it as the most important lifelong commitment in our lives. Remember that no matter how mature, successful, or strong we are in our adult lives, we are still the children of our parents. Thus, we should maintain the behavior learned in our childhood — to live dutifully and behave respectfully in the presence of our kind and loving parents. Their kindness can only be repaid by being humble, respectful, dutiful, obedient, and by fulfilling their hopes and wishes. We should listen to them carefully for their words of wisdom and advice, and honor them through our actions and thoughts, making sure that their needs are met, as they made sure our needs were met when we were young. We should provide them with comfort, especially in their older years, and never go against their words and wishes. By doing so, the natural relationship becomes meritorious, which brings joy in the parents' hearts and success in their children's lives.

It can be beneficial to consider other cultures' perspectives regarding relationships between parents and children, as we can certainly gain some understanding of different ways to view things. In the Tibetan culture, parents have traditionally been worthy of trust and respect, being the main source of moral guidance as their children's first teachers. Parents have been the most important part of Tibetan home life; the ultimate bond between parent and child. Tibetan parents have predominately been considered as revered and above everyone else in terms of the kindness, care, love, affection, and guidance given to their children. Additionally, Tibetan parents serve as a source of blessings, success, and all other virtues in their children's lives. Tibetans recognize that this reverence cannot be measured or repaid in this life through any means apart from being humble, respectful, and honoring one's parents in both thoughts and actions. Sadly, this deep understanding is undergoing change in Tibetan families in the modern world. As a result, more Tibetan parents and children live in broken relationships that bring unhappiness on both sides. This needs to be corrected immediately before it is too late.

In Indian culture, people have customarily regarded their parents as having the highest status in the family, to be worthy of love, veneration, respect, and reverence by their children. Children, including adult children, would hold this view for their entire lifetime. Unfortunately, this deference and appreciation for parents have evolved over time. Nowadays, many parents and children have become unhappier because the natural relationship between the parents and children has changed. This bond was primarily severed and abandoned in the hearts of the children.

We may believe that the cause of these changes in children's behavior is due to times having changed, i.e., gotten more modern. But in reality, we humans have changed, not the times. We are becoming more immoral, ungrateful, self-centered, and materialistic as opposed to being humane and civilized. We are indeed changing, not the times. We must not blame our societal problems on the times; instead, we should blame ourselves and make sure to rectify our own behaviors.

~ ~ ~ ~ ~

In our modern world, when most people think about relationships, they tend to dwell on love and friendship relationships. Interest in family relationships are often more about searching for your ancestry through a DNA analysis. There is little interest in spending more time with parents, siblings, or aunts and uncles. We are told that to be happy, we need to have many close friends and find the perfect partner to share our lives with. Since the advent of the Internet, more and more people seek their true love from online services, introducing them to complete strangers who match their specified profile. Parents and other family members often have no background knowledge whatsoever of the chosen partner, nor have any input in the decision-making process. Love and friendship relationships are of the utmost importance to many people in today's world. But what about the relationship with our birth family? Are they to be treated as strangers, or cast aside as not needed any longer? After all, being adults allows us to do as we choose. However, the idea of being grownup has limitations, as we shall see, since the parent/child relationship must be nurtured and protected in many ways for us to fulfill our duties and be truly happy.

Among all types of associations, the natural relationship between parents and children is the most sacred and profound by nature, and this relationship needs to be cherished through all means. Children who disregard or disrespect this relationship will lead them to have many unexpected problems and tragedies in their lives. Therefore, it is extremely important for children not to ignore or disdain the natural relationship with their parents. In turn, parents should not abandon their love towards their children until the relationship ends at death.

Because of the innate, pure, and natural relationship between parents and their children, children who lie, deceive, show disrespect, keep secrets, use harsh words, disregard their parent's words, go against their parent's will, or steal from their parents are displaying extremely negative and detrimental behaviors. These actions will ultimately cause the loss of genuine happiness and success in the children's lives. This is because the sacred natural relationship has been severed and the parents' loving hearts have been injured by the negative behaviors of their children. Concerning telling lies and falsehoods, children lying to their parents in any manner is by nature one of the worst forms of lying.

A child, or adult child, displaying bias and favoritism towards one parent is also very negative and can lead to serious implications for the family. For example, being very close to one's mother by sharing thoughts, information, and being in complete agreement, while being distant and not agreeable to one's father is highly negative and unreasonable misbehavior. Some natural undesirable consequences in the child's life may include alienation, prejudice, and misinterpretation of the truth, not thinking of other viewpoints, and fracturing the parent/child bond. The child may also suffer mentally, emotionally, psychologically, or in their worldly tasks in terms of undergoing difficulties to succeed in their endeavors. Children and adult children need to understand that a parent's love, support, advice, and suggestions in whatever they attempt to do plays a positive key role in the child's success. Children who do not place enough value in the words and thoughts of their parents may not have a good chance to succeed or find genuine happiness in any aspect of their lives. These potential outcomes are based on the natural relationship that is sacred to children as well as their parents.

Having a good, loving, healthy relationship with our parents will continue to nurture us throughout our lives, just as our mother's milk and parents' hugs nurtured us as babies. By holding on to a bond of unconditional love from parents to children, and children being respectful, humble, and dutiful to their parents in sickness and in old age, the relationship will survive and prosper. While it is important to honor this relationship, it should not be thought of in a religious sense, but rather in a conventional sense of a good and healthy connection that serves as a source of joy and success for all. This relationship is not created by God or by anyone else. Instead, a link is established by the interaction and deeply involved emotions between the potential parents and their potential child. In other words, the link is established through the connection of the sperm, the egg, and the consciousness that uses the sperm and egg to form the offspring's physical body. The consciousness enters the mixture of the sperm and egg like a tourist checks into a hotel room. Based on this link, we inherit our body from our parents as a house or shell to temporarily live in — perhaps seventy to eighty years or so. We claim our parent's sperm and egg as our own body and therefore become very attached to our body. In reality, our body is our inheritance and our parents are our forbearers.

Keeping this in mind, children should live with a clear recognition of their parents based on destiny, instead of parents as friends. I have often met people who declare: *My mother (or my father) is my best friend.* It truly shocked me at first and made me contemplate on that concept for a while. I honestly realized that parents are much more than a friend could ever be, and the kindness, caring, and love of parents for their children cannot be compared to friendship. Therefore, always dwell on the kindness of your parents, be humble and respectful towards them, and be willing to repay their kindness. Be vigilant about the needs of your parents and make sure to provide for their comfort and safety. Stay in close contact with them, regardless of where you live and what you do. Do not ever think of your parents as a ladder for you to climb in order to reach your full potential in adulthood. I have met numerous people who to some extent have abandoned their parents by having little or no contact with them. I found them to be unhappy people, with less stability and little success in their lives. Their unhappiness and failures can most likely be related to the natural consequences of severing the natural relationship ties between parents and their children. Make sure to know that a good relationship bond, formed with unconditional love and respect between parents and their children, is one of the most important sources of happiness, stability, and success.

~ ~ ~ ~ ~

Many responsibilities need to be fulfilled by both parents and children. Some of the primary ones for parents include the following:

- Be parents, not babysitters.
- Teach by example.
- Give full attention to your child's needs.
- Awaken your child's mind to the importance of ethics and inner moral qualities.
- Help reduce the desire for unnecessary possessions, money, and social image.
- Be present while your child does his/her homework.
- At bedtime, help your child prepare his/her mind for the next day.
- Always watch your child's behavior for warning signs of problems.
- Guard against your child befriending children with bad behaviors.
- Explain to your child the consequences of actions and behaviors, rather than simply stating, "do not do that."

For children, including adult children, the primary responsibilities include:

- Never lie, deceive, or keep secrets from your parents.
- Never show disrespect or disregard your parent's words.
- Do not go against your parent's will.
- Never steal from your parents.
- Do not display bias or favoritism towards one parent.
- Always be respectful, humble, and dutiful to your parents.
- Dwell on the kindness of your parents.

- As an adult child, provide for your parents' comfort and safety.
- Always stay in close contact with your parents.

To summarize, society seems to have lost an understanding of what a parent's role needs to be to raise their children in a wholesome way. Parents are not just part-time babysitters; they need to give full attention to their children. By focusing on the quality of their children's lives, and the quality of the relationship between the parents and their children, more positive outcomes should ensue. Many people believe that children of wealthy parents are in a better situation to provide their children with the necessary possessions to have a happy childhood. However, the most important things to give children are love, affection, attention, ethical and moral guidance, and a good education.

The child's role in the family is also very important. Children need to respect their parents and fulfill their moral duties to them. Children also should understand the importance of education, and the effort required to be a good student. Without appreciating how important and necessary their parents are in their upbringing, children are often mentally lost and fearful of the future.

The family unit needs to be united for the household to function in a strong and healthy way. Everyone in the family plays an important role in making this happen. We cannot allow the ills and changes in society to work like a contagious disease and spread negative conditions to adults and especially to our innocent children. Our society can be badly affected by these negative social conditions if our children do not have strong, well-founded, self-disciplined, and proper ethical guidance.

CHAPTER 4

Parents' Moral Responsibilities Regarding Their Children

T HE NATURAL RELATIONSHIP bond between parents and their children carries with it certain obligations and accountabilities. One is a moral responsibility towards the child, which should be carried out from the time of conception through to maturity. It is easy to understand what a responsibility is, such as making sure our car has required inspections, paying our taxes on time, and washing the dirty dishes. But what exactly is a *moral* responsibility? Morality can mean different things to different people, but in general, morality may include right or wrong and good or bad behaviors. However, morality, in the sense of our moral duty towards our children, cannot be limited to right vs. wrong or good vs. bad. Rather, morality is the need to analyze and consider in all situations what is the better action, and what outcomes may occur due to our decisions.

This may seem like an impossible or even an unnecessary task, but what could be more important than to deliberate over how we raise our children? We may begin by asking ourselves some basic questions, such as: *What do I want my child to become?, What are the most beneficial things for my child to learn?, How can I help my child to achieve these things?, What can I do to help my child become a wholesome, successful adult?* As society becomes more complex, often with less family unity, we may fail to see the ramifications of not raising children in a more moral way. The unwholesome and unhappy outcomes that we are observing more frequently in our children and young adults affect not only the children and parents, but also society as a whole.

Being a parent is certainly not an easy task, particularly in our current world. Parenthood carries with it demanding moral responsibilities relating to the upbringing of children and securing their future well-being. Children are bound to suffer when their parents fail to meet these duties due to selfishness, negligence, or being unaware of their moral obligations. In contemporary times, quite a few young parents do not seem to be paying full attention to how their actions are affecting their children's well-being. Animals instinctively know how to safeguard their offspring in order to have a good chance of survival, i.e., to stay alive until mature enough to survive on their own. While many animals are adept at knowing how to care for their young, they do not have the capacity to ensure their offspring's future well-being. Human parents, on the other hand, have the intellectual acumen and moral responsibility to be knowledgeable and discerning about the upbringing of their children in order to help ensure their future welfare and nourish the natural parent-child relationship.

It is evident that some parents are not fully engaged with their children. A parent may be holding a beer bottle in one hand, a cigarette in the other hand, and chit chatting with someone while their baby is crying in a stroller. Or, their young child is about to cross a busy street, while their parent is immersed in something on their smart phone, taking no notice of the situation. A heartbreaking occurrence, which seems to be happening more frequently, is when a busy parent rushes off to work, leaving their baby in the back of the car. Later in the day, the baby is found slumped over in their car seat, having died from heat exhaustion. Sadly, this is not a freak incident — these tragedies are recurrently reported on the news nowadays. In all of these and other cases, the child sorely needed his or her parent's attention. Even if an incident does not end tragically, the love bond established at birth between the parent and child can be damaged. A sense of being left out or even abandoned can begin to form in the child's mind, which can affect the parent-child relationship, and eventually the child's ethical conduct and healthy social behaviors.

An initial and important part of being engaged in the moral upbringing of a child is to recognize the child's natural predisposition, sensitivities, and flexibility in order to effectively help meet the child's individual needs for healthy development. Not being able to identify these unique traits can result in the parent being harsh, rigid, or misunderstanding the child's behavior. These errors in parental judgment can be very damaging to the child, as the young one may become frustrated and unable to develop self-confidence, social skills, learning strategies, and other abilities. Each child has distinct inclinations which, when nurtured wisely and kindly, can kindle a sense of freedom in the child's mind, allowing him or her to learn skills more quickly and easily.

Another moral responsibility of parents is to spend more time with their children, especially when they are young. Infants and young children yearn for their parents' attention and physical comfort. Soothing words, loving hugs, and listening to what the child is saying are extremely important and a critical factor in the child's development. Fulfilling this need is like fertilizer to a plant — it will help the child grow and thrive, both mentally and physically. The lack of the parent's attention and comfort can harm the overall wellbeing of the child. One note of caution — spending more time literally means more time, not just "quality time" of a short duration.

Even when children are babies, parents should spend a good amount of time reading to them and telling them stories. By using facial expressions and an animated and soothing voice, the baby will become more engaged and interested. When the child is old enough to understand, short moral and ethical tales can leave lasting impressions in the child's mind. Telling young children simple pleasant jokes can lead to warmth and laughter between parents and their children. Young children also love to draw and color, and that doesn't mean that parents can't join in and color as well. Household activities and chores can be added at an appropriate age. Planting flowers and vegetables is educational and fun, while helping with cooking and collecting the trash helps a child to learn that he or she is part of the family unit in sharing responsibilities.

All of these activities help children to form a close, loving bond with their parents. To help make daily tasks more amenable, a parent could explain why it is important to clean the dishes. The parent may say: *When there is something to eat, then there will always be some work to be done. Someone who likes to eat, but does not like to cook, do the dishes, or clean up the kitchen is creating a big problem. We are a happy family and we do not want that problem in our home. No one other than our family will do the dishes for us, and we should not let the dishes sit in the sink for days. We all like to eat on clean plates, drink with clean cups and glasses, and cook with clean pots. Don't you think so ...my son or daughter?* In the beginning a child may say: *I do not want to do the dishes!* But gradually the child will join with the parents to help cook, do the dishes, clean the kitchen, and put things away. He or she will have a feeling of accomplishment, especially if the parents express their feelings of happiness.

Acquiring these types of skills can help children to learn self-discipline and responsibility in the home, which can lead to the same practices at school and eventually at work. Parents need to make certain that children understand that all family members have rights and responsibilities for as long as they live in the family home. Every family member has the right to claim their own dues, but at the same time every family member has a duty to fulfill their responsibilities. Parents should teach these fundamental principles to their children and make certain that they truly understand the meanings of rights and responsibilities. Once the concept of rights and responsibilities are concrete, children can carry these traits to their schools and eventually to the wider community, thus creating room for joy, happiness, and progress in the world.

Alongside behavioral instructions is a more subtle form of parental moral responsibility. It is of utmost importance to ensure that a natural and healthy relationship bond develops between parents and their children. Without this, a close and intimate connection cannot foster and grow. To achieve this requires a great deal of observation and instinct to discover the uniqueness of each child and how he/she relates to their parents. This involves discussing with children what parents really are, what children really are, and each other's role in the family. In addition, children need to learn how this parent/child relationship evolves from birth until death, as the child will eventually become an adult. At first, it may seem a bit strange to think that we need to teach children about this relationship. However, especially in our modern times when many families are not close physically or emotionally, this concept needs to be taught in order to be fully understood.

One way in which parents can begin to understand each of their children's separate and unique attributes and needs is by carefully observing each child's intellectual, mental, and physical abilities and traits. For example, you begin to notice that your child is not interested in reading books and you are concerned that this may hinder their educational progress. What steps could you take once you observe this tendency? First, you could be a good role model by reading more books in the presence of your child. If age appropriate, you could share some things you found interesting in the books and discuss them with your child. Another strategy is for both of you to read the same book, similar to a "book club". You could then set up meeting times to discuss each chapter. Talking honestly with your child about their lack of interest in reading can also be beneficial, as this may lead to better understanding your child's feelings about reading. Once you start talking openly with your child, this may naturally progress to you and your child discussing other issues and thoughts throughout your lifetime.

Another example concerns physical abilities or interests. If you see that your child is not comfortable or willing to engage in certain physical activities, such as swimming, do not give up hope that your child cannot learn to swim. In addition to taking your child to swimming lessons and watching from the side of the pool, take time to go swimming with your child, ideally on a regular basis. Even if you are not a swimmer, you and your child can both learn to put your face in the water and start to feel more comfortable. You can ask your child why learning to swim is important and beneficial. Being honest and sharing with your child that you regret not learning to swim as a child can be supportive and comforting.

Often people may believe that it is best to learn from one's mistakes. From the time we are quite young, we hear this over and over again. Here are a few quotes from famous people that illustrate this belief:

You will only fail to learn if you do not learn from failing.
—STELLA ADLER

You don't learn to walk by following rules. You learn by doing, and by falling over.
—RICHARD BRANSON

While this type of thinking may be useful in some cases, we often use this rationale as an excuse for our poor decisions. We may mistakenly think that it is not only okay to fail and make mistakes, but that we must do so in order for us to learn — by ourselves.

There is, however, another and often better choice. In our individualistic society, we are surrounded by this concept; that we need to stand on our own two feet, be independent, and not ask for any advice or help. But *asking for help*, such as money or other forms of monetary help, especially when not truly needed, is not the same as *asking for advice*. This yearning for independence, including not listening to elders/parents, not asking or taking advice, and doing whatever we decide to do, is often harmful to both children and parents, and to society in general.

The following account is an example of this type of thinking. A very nice young woman recently completed an associate degree in Nursing. Because her family had modest income, she attended a community college, as the cost was much less than at a university. To save more money, she also lived at home, rather than in a dormitory or an apartment. These decisions were made by her parents, with her agreement and understanding. However, as soon as she graduated from the program, she decided on her own to move to an apartment with a friend. She was now a grownup, had a nursing degree, and did not want to live at home any longer. To pay the rent and living expenses, she took a job as a waitress, which required her to work long hours to earn enough money to survive. She knew that as soon as she passed the Nursing Board exams, she would earn much more money. So, she believed that all was going to work out very well. Then, something happened that she did not plan on. She did not pass the Nursing Board exams. Part of the reason she failed was because she was working day and night at her waitressing job, and had little time left to study diligently. She is now facing a dilemma. She cannot go back to live with her parents, as she signed a year's lease on the apartment. She must continue to work long hours to pay her living expenses. She cannot ask her parents for a loan, as their income is very low. The outcome to her situation is unknown. However, if she had sincerely and humbly asked her parents or a knowledgeable adult for advice, she may have decided to stay at home and study for the exam. Unfortunately, her desire for independence got in the way of her rational thinking.

If children are raised with an understanding of the importance of having a comfortable and intimate relationship with their parents, the outcome for many adult children will likely be positive. One word of advice: parents need to be the parents, and not have children give advice to their parents. Unfortunately, advice-giving by children to their parents is becoming a common theme on television programs and advertisements. With that conflicted view, children, teenagers, and young adults may not readily ask their parents for any advice, even when it is truly needed.

The advent of the technology age has had an enormous impact, both good and bad, on society. At the micro-level (the family), the influences of the Internet and personal devices may be more harmful than initially realized. Parents have a daunting task to be the guardians of their children, especially when the predator may appear to be invisible or innocuous. Children are being exposed to electronic devices at a very early age, as now companies are marketing these tools for small children in the form of computers, touch screen activity desks, tablets, cameras, and smart watches. It is very difficult for bicycles, group sports, board games, playmates, or even parents to compete with these enticements. Even more concerning is how staring at a screen for periods of time can be damaging to the eyes, mental health, and beneficial social interactions. The human mind seems to gravitate more easily towards a device rather than towards a human.

For many years, television has played a part in everyday life for children. On the positive side, there were, and still are, programs geared to children's interests, including educational programs. Before 24-hour cable services became the norm, children would seek other forms of entertainment once a TV program was over. Nowadays, television is truly a twenty-four-hour daily event, with cable, streaming platforms, and all sorts of other ways to watch TV. With this almost unlimited access to TV, parents need to be vigilant about the amount of time their children are spending watching TV shows.

All of the above forms of entertainment can easily lead to a sort of addiction, a dependence that can cancel out normal human interactions and brain functioning. When a person binge watches TV, plays video games endlessly, or a touchscreen device continuously, the brain may produce dopamine. The person can then experience a drug-like high that makes the user crave the activity more and more. It is the pleasure of the activity that promotes this addiction, similar to other addictions. Truly worrisome is that young children can suffer from the effects of these types of activities. Parents need to recognize the danger and consider what their moral responsibility is to combat this serious problem. Parents should ask themselves: *Is cable TV really necessary and is it helping or harming my children? What effects will my young child have when sitting with an electronic toy for long periods of time? Am I honestly buying these devices to better my child's life, or to use them as a babysitter?*

~ ~ ~ ~ ~

Parents need to be their children's first teacher, with the home being the first school in their children's world. Parents need to realize this indisputable fact and make certain to carry out this duty to the fullest extent possible. Some parents may believe that they are not qualified to be their child's teacher, but they certainly are capable and play a vital role in preparing their children for formal schooling. There are several key components that parents should teach their children to prepare them for school. These are the types of skills and habits that most certainly will facilitate the transition to formal schooling for your children.

Important note: All children, from birth on up, need several hours of one-on-one interaction with their parents (or another adult) daily to develop the necessary skills for school readiness.

The following items are categorized into four areas. None of these cost any money, except perhaps for a few board games. Therefore, this truly is a free education, paid for by a parent's love and ethical devotion.

Grooming and hygiene

- Make certain your child is completely toilet trained by the time they begin kindergarten (if not earlier).
- Your child should be taught to wash their hands after using the toilet.

- He/she should be able to comb their hair and brush their teeth.
- They need to be able to dress themselves, put on coats and boots, and use buttons, zippers, and Velcro closings as needed. If your child has shoes with laces, they need to learn how to tie them.

Emotional and behavioral readiness

- Teach your child to follow directions (for example, to put an object in a certain place — *Please put this spoon in the top drawer*).
- Teach listening skills and not to interrupt (you, the teacher, or others who are talking, including other children).
- Practice sitting still for a length of time (begin with a few minutes at a time, without being occupied with anything — TV, music, video games, talking, etc.).
- Learn how to wait to use the toilet (for a reasonable amount of time — 5 minutes or so).
- Learn how to share with others and not to grab something from them.
- Learn how to be empathic to others (with kind words and gestures).
- Learn proper composure and how to hold emotions in check.

Proper eating habits and manners

- Teach your child to use cutlery correctly (how to hold and use a knife, fork, and spoon).
- While eating with others, wait for everyone to begin eating together.
- Learn how to pass food around the table to others.
- Develop good eating manners (eating with the mouth closed, not talking while eating, and not putting too much food in the mouth at one time).

- Help your child develop tastes for various healthy foods, and not be a picky eater.
- Teach your child to use a tissue for a runny nose, and never to blow your nose at a table while people are eating (step aside to do that in private).

Learning preparedness

- Expose your young child to paper books (not just electronic versions).
- Provide picture books for your young child to "read" to themselves.
- Read books to your child to develop a love for reading and listening skills.
- Play educational board games with your child.
- Teach your child to speak in full sentences.
- Teach your child to understand descriptive, full sentences (questions, explanations, concepts).
- Make sure your child gets a good night's sleep every night (8 — 10 hours of uninterrupted sleep in a quiet room).

To aid in this effort, the home should be conducive for children to learn these basic skills and help prepare them for school. A clean and organized home environment contributes to the well-being of everyone in the family. While the house need not be spotless, it should be tidy and clean. Keeping dangerous items away from a young child's reach is also important. A child-safe home will not only be less risky but will also avoid having the child hear: *No, don't touch!* all of the time. Frequently making statements like this may harm a child's growing self-confidence, interest in learning, and curiosity. It can also damage the parent and child natural bond, as negative words may sound threatening and fearful to a young child. Instead of saying *"No"*, parents should explain situations in a simple and straightforward way. Look for what the child may be doing correctly and guide him or her in that direction with encouraging words, such as *"great"* or *"so good"*.

Once children are in school, the home still plays an important function in their education, as at the end of the day children bring home what they have learned at school. The parent's moral responsibility again comes into play, by nurturing the child's interest in their education. To help retain what the child has been taught at school each day, the parent's role is to help their child understand, absorb, and retain the teachings, as well as to prepare for the next day's lessons.

~ ~ ~ ~ ~

The work of education is divided between the
teacher and the environment.

—MARIA MONTESSORI

Finding an appropriate school, geared to the needs of the individual child, should be every parent's legitimate moral responsibility. At the same time, it is important for parents to facilitate their children's learning and knowledge acquisition by monitoring homework assignments and preparation for exams at home. This creates a cohesive entity — student, teacher, and parents, who support each other's efforts regarding the child's education. Leaving children's education solely in the hands of the school is unwise. Practicing self-discipline and having a home atmosphere conducive to learning are key factors for children to become better students. Parents must actively participate in their children's education, making sure that their children are indeed *learning* at school. By regularly checking with the teacher about their child's learning skills and conduct, parents may be able to intercept and correct detrimental behaviors before it is too late. Parents, more than teachers, may be aware of their child's inclinations, which can help to remedy a situation quickly. To state this once more — it is every parent's moral responsibility to nurture their children's education at home in order for their children to be successful in school.

Every child is unique in many ways, and both parents and teachers should respond to each child according to the child's learning abilities and natural skills. Pressuring a child too firmly may thwart the child's desire to learn, like breaking the backbone of a camel by putting an elephant on the camel's back. I strongly recommend that all parents and teachers never use this strategy on children. I remember that I lost my desire to study and learn for a few weeks when I was in my late teens at my monastery. My teacher pushed weighty philosophical concepts on me compassionately, albeit relentlessly, and my mind was about to crack into pieces under the constant pressure.

Parents and teachers should bear in mind that education, discipline, and good behavior go hand in hand, with all three being complementary to each other. Good behavior and discipline play an important role in every child's life, as a quality education without good behavior will have little worth in a person's personal life or in society. Children with behavioral difficulties and a lack of discipline cannot learn very well at school, as their poor behavior at home may carry over into the classroom. The discipline learned from parents needs to develop into self-discipline, self-control, and orderliness. Parents need to set guidelines concerning home discipline (does not mean "punishment") to help create an atmosphere that is as calm and pleasant as possible. Family disputes, talking loudly, and yelling are upsetting to everyone, especially innocent young children. Even minor negative actions, such as playing loud music or having the TV on most of the time can interrupt anyone's concentration. As a result, children may have difficulty learning to focus their minds and may not pay attention very well in school. It is also advisable to have adequate space in the home for children's school supplies and books. A desk or table and bookshelf in a quiet area can guide children to their "learning place" in the home.

Once children begin formal schooling, they may be exposed to undesirable conduct from some children. This may happen at school, on school buses, or other places where children are not under the supervision of their parents or another adult. Along with being exposed to negative actions at school, "hangout" places can be breeding grounds for children and teenagers to learn detrimental things from others who influence them, often in the name of "friendship". Parents need to be aware of the dangers of these situations and the effects they can have on their children. We have all probably witnessed parents who drop off their elementary or middle school children at school well before opening time. The children then mingle with other kids with little or no supervision. Parents may go to work, to exercise, or call friends to meet for coffee while their children may be adopting negative behaviors from other children. Regardless of the reason for not taking or picking children up at the correct time, parents should make arrangements to have their children cared for by a responsible adult in such cases.

Another issue parents may face with school-aged children and teenagers is the popularity of sleepovers. The practice of having sleepovers is actually not very beneficial or worthwhile, as they can easily turn into a free-for-all party that lasts all night. At sleepovers, children unquestionably stay up very late; likely until well after midnight without anyone watching to see what TV programs or movies they are watching, what types of games they are playing, or what they are talking about. With teens, or even pre-teens, sleepovers can lead to drinking alcohol, smoking cigarettes or even taking drugs in the home while the parents are sound asleep. The most common "innocent" things that children may do at sleepovers are to have pillow fights, make a mess, watch TV, videos, or movies endlessly, and do things that are not typically allowed in their own homes.

Some, or perhaps many American parents may believe that sleepovers are simply a part of the American culture and are therefore acceptable. But have these parents critically thought about the possible ramifications of this custom? By and large, it can become risky when "bad ideas and bad habits" become part of a culture. Similarly, it can become dangerous when the culture becomes part of religion, the religion becomes part of politics, and then politics becomes part of corruption. Other societies have comparable problems, albeit in different forms. In some cultures, boys may be given a weapon, such as a gun or knife, as a mark of developing manhood.

In many Asian and European countries, parents may give alcohol to their children at a very young age, particularly during holidays or festivals. While these may be considered customary and even important in some cultures, parents should analyze these practices to determine if they truly are in the best interest of their children. Parents need to be wiser and more skillful, rather than simply following customs and traditions when it comes to their children's well-being and moral conduct.

In this day and age, birthday parties are commonplace for children and adults alike. Deciding whether to have birthday parties for children is something that needs to be carefully thought through and discussed by parents. Mom and dad should not feel obligated to have a birthday party every year for their children, regardless of what the neighbors or friends think. Likewise, children should not feel entitled to have birthday parties given in their honor. Several considerations worth discussing may include the following; the first two involve discussions with the child:

- What is the true meaning and intent of having a birthday party? (Discuss with child.)
- Why is it good or beneficial to have, or not to have a birthday party? (Discuss with child.)
- How many people should be invited? (Parents to decide.)
- Should only close family members and close friends be invited to the party? (Parents to decide.)
- Where should the party be held — at home or a party venue? (Parents to decide.)
- How much will the party cost, and can we afford the cost? (Parents to decide.)
- If parents cannot afford to have a birthday party for the child, what other options are there to celebrate the child's birthday? (Parents to decide with child.)

Celebrating a child's birthday with close family and friends, who are sharing love and a sense of joy over his or her birth is certainly good and there is nothing wrong in doing so. Having a small and simple birthday party is best, as boosting a child's ego can be more damaging than not having a party at all. Many parents strive to have the biggest party they can, with many guests who bring numerous gifts. This situation makes for too much excitement, with the child concentrating on all of their presents and a big cake. Instead, along with a few well-chosen gifts, parents could start or add to a savings account in the child's name to use in the future for their education or other important things. Parents could also suggest that the invitees contribute a small dollar amount to the child's savings account in lieu of bringing presents. One final suggestion would be to dismiss the party altogether and take the group of invitees to do something charitable — for the elderly, homeless animals, or the environment, and celebrate with cake and ice cream at the end of the day.

Perhaps everyone, not only parents, should think about the prevalence of having birthday parties in our culture. Nowadays, college students and young adults often celebrate their birthdays by going out partying and drinking with friends or making sure to see how many birthday wishes they received on Facebook. Not all that long ago, birthday parties were primarily for young children, and typically ended once the child reached middle school. Other occasions to hold birthday parties were for elderly relatives, perhaps a grandparent who reached age 80 or 90. These were special events and made birthday parties a celebration of life. Maybe we all should reconsider what is the true purpose of having birthday parties and begin to have them for more meaningful milestones.

~ ~ ~ ~ ~

Once children reach a certain age, they are considered as adults in legal terms. There are specific criteria, depending on the category and the state in which a person lives for the age of majority, age of consent, age of criminal responsibility, voting age, drinking age, and driving age. For many parents, high school graduation is the beginning of adulthood with some, if not all, independence and liberation from their parents or guardians. In modern times, sending children away to college rather than going to a college close to home has become common. Once their son or daughter arrives at the school, parents may seldom see or even have much contact with their offspring. Parents may believe that since they are now young adults, they will or should be able to cope on their own and learn from their own mistakes. But parents should ask themselves: *Does an 18-year-old suddenly become a responsible adult the day they graduate from high school?*

College campuses nowadays are a far cry from how they were a generation or so ago. Today, college students have many more freedoms and responsibilities. Dormitories most likely have fewer rules or regulations, with no curfews or "house mothers" to watch over the students to see who is entering or leaving the residence halls. Many dorms are unisex, with males and females sharing adjacent rooms and bathrooms in close proximity to each other. Alcohol is often permitted in residence halls, with an often-disregarded stipulation that only 21-year-olds are permitted to imbibe. Alongside the lack of curfews, many schools allow students, including freshmen, to have their own cars on campus. With few restrictions in the dorms, 18-year-olds may stay out all night, with no one knowing their whereabouts. Even inside the dorms, parties, drinking, drugs, and other risky behaviors are commonplace. In addition, many young students have credit cards, which can lead to irresponsible spending. The sense of freedom in allowing these things is appealing to young adults, even if they have been brought up by responsible parents. It is not easy to say no to these temptations, as students want and need to make friends and be involved in college life.

With an understanding of the situation on many college campuses, what are parents to do? First, it is wise to find out as much as possible about the campus' culture, including what activities are permitted and the specific campus regulations for students to abide by. Parents can also access the college's crime data reports in the campus police office to analyze their data. This knowledge is as important in selecting the college your child will attend as to how academically sound the school is. Next, parents need to be honest and frank with their son or daughter about how challenging and potentially dangerous the "freedom" of living away from home can be. It may be helpful to show them details of incidents on college campuses to alert them of the dangers and explain the possible consequences of participating in some of these activities. The more parents and children are aware and honest with each other, the better. Keep in mind that undergraduate students typically take five courses per semester, which is approximately only 15 hours of time in class per week. That means that college students have a great amount of time outside the classroom in which to occupy their time — for better or for worse.

During the school year, parents and their children should make sure to stay in contact by calling each other on a regular basis. Calling is much better than texting, as humans need to communicate with their senses. Parents have a right and a responsibility to know how their college student is doing in their classes, social lives, with their budget, and if they are having any problems. Young adults may believe that talking with their parents about their lives is being immature. However, it is a sign of *maturity* to be able to discuss issues with parents. Parents need to explain to their son or daughter that rather than *learning from your mistakes,* young adults should ask for advice from their parents. If young adults understand this concept, it can certainly help to avoid problems in the future.

College students often depend on and trust friends for advice regarding serious issues, thus taking over the role of parental responsibility and guidance. This is sadly prevalent in our modern, individualistic, and self-centered world. Young adults, who know their parents and whose parents know them far better than newly found friends, often rely on these "strangers" for weighty and far-reaching answers to problems and moral dilemmas, while discarding their parent's wisdom, love, and understanding. We all need friends, and companionship can offer happiness and lend a helping hand with daily matters. But we should never misunderstand the meaning of friendship and confuse it with "parentship".

Modern science has indicated that the human brain does not fully mature, especially for males, until age 25 to 30. Yet, we allow our young people to believe that they are mature adults, in part by giving them their own cars (sometimes as early as 16 years old), credit cards, and many freedoms, especially on college campuses. Drugs, drinking in excess, casual sex, staying out all night, and living with a boyfriend or girlfriend have become commonplace in today's youth culture. Too many of these risky behaviors have led to failures, tragedies, and unfixable mistakes. This happens at Ivy League universities as well as state schools and small colleges. Can we allow our society to believe that in this "modern" complex world, an 18-year-old should have completely free rein? Should we just send our 18-year-olds away to college, cross our fingers, close our eyes, and hope for the best? Parents have abdicated their responsibilities to the colleges, and colleges (which used to have *in loco parentis* policies) have abdicated their responsibilities to the students. The result is that now students are permitted to do almost anything they choose.

Not so long ago, teenagers and young adults typically did not own cars until they completed their schooling and secured a fulltime job. And, they certainly did not have credit cards to spend money at will. These, and the freedoms on college campuses are not helping young people become responsible, mature adults. The Minimum Legal Drinking Age (MLDA) set by the U.S. government is now age 21. Many states have also raised the legal smoking age to 21. These are indeed good actions by government. However, they are not adequate measures to advance the well-being of our youth. Ironically, birthday parties and dressing up for Halloween used to be solely for children, who usually stopped wanting to do these things by the end of elementary school. Now, these parties are also for adults, where they engage in child-like behaviors. Our society has twisted things around, which has led to confusion; adult behaviors in children and teens, and child-like behavior in adults.

We do not own our children, as everyone grows up to be an independent adult. However, parents do have moral responsibilities to fulfill until their children are fully grown and at the age of majority.

Likewise, children have responsibilities to their parents as well. This does not mean earning a degree from a highly rated university or securing a prestigious or well-paying job. It means having learned from their parents to have good manners, ethical behaviors, deference to elders, and kindness and consideration for others. Where else can children learn these most important skills than from their parents?

We can use the analogy of a mother bird, who constantly watches over her chicks, making sure they are protected, well fed, and being taught to fly. The mother bird helps her chicks to build strength in their wings and to learn ways of finding food so that the chicks develop the know-how to survive. Only then can the mother bird send her chicks away from the nest with few concerns, fears, or worries about their future. Human beings should be able to do as much, if not far more, than what other creatures do in raising their offspring in a moral and highly principled manner.

In closing, parents should make sure that their relationship with their children is in being a *parent* and not a *friend*. There is a meaningful difference between being a parent and being a friend, and the two should not be mixed together. A parent should be the one to help with their child's mental and emotional well-being and psychological balance by providing the nourishment of love, compassion, and a deep sense of intimacy. Opening the child's mind to appreciating the true importance of patience, respect, honesty, sincerity, and a sense of contentment with what one has can only be taught by a parent. This is not the purview of a friend. Sometimes parents may attempt to influence and shape their children's thoughts about the importance of wealth and social standing, believing that this is the path to happiness and success. These values can ultimately lead to unhappiness and selfishness, with a sense of isolation and loneliness. Parents need to recognize that their child's future happiness and success should not be defined by the *quantity* of the possessions they have, but rather by the *quality* of their mind and how they relate to the world.

CHAPTER 5

Children's Moral Responsibilities Regarding Their Elderly Parents

Please note: In this chapter, we are examining the obligations and importance that adult children need to recognize and carry out regarding the person or persons who cared for and raised them from the time they were born until adulthood. There are people who have not been brought up at home with a parent, relative, or guardian. These children may have been cared for and raised in an orphanage or group home for children. Others may have had their parent or parents pass away and were cared for by others for a period of time. If this, or something similar was the case, the information and recommendations in this chapter may not be applicable in all cases.

I N THIS CONTEXT, the term "parent" or "parents" refers to the primary caregiver(s) — the person or persons who were responsible for your upbringing. "Morality" means holding your parents in high regard with respect, humility, and a voluntary willingness to support and assist them whenever they are in need of help. This may include in their old age, when sick, weak, or lacking material necessities for their comfort, safety, and general well-being.

Many of us are parents, but we all have been children. Often, our memories do not serve us well, and we may have forgotten all of the compassionate loving care, noble guidance, unrelenting attention, self-sacrificing monetary outlays, and hard work our parents were engaged in while raising us to adulthood. Therefore, in this chapter we will strive to refresh our memories and offer sound and humble advice about caring for our parents once we reach adulthood.

When we leave our parent's home, either to attend college, join the military, or find a job and move into our own apartment, we often are elated that we are finally liberated from our parents. We yearn to be fully-fledged adults, with the freedom to live how we want to live, think how we want to think, and do what we want to do. No longer should our parents tell us not to drink alcohol or smoke cigarettes, when to come home at night, what to eat, who to date, or anything else. If and when we decide to marry, we may think about starting our own family, apart from the family who raised us. We've found the "love of our life" and believe that we should devote ourselves solely to this one person. We are now so busy with our spouse that we don't seem to have the time or even an interest in going to visit our parents or call them on the phone.

In all of these cases, we may believe that we do not need, or sometimes do not even want our parents to be involved in our lives any longer. In some respects, this may be appropriate. We certainly should clean our own homes, wash our own clothes, do our own grocery shopping, and pay our own bills. Nor should we seek financial help from our parents, unless agreed upon in certain legitimate circumstances. With these types of things, we absolutely should be independent from our parents.

However, our definition of independence may not take into account how our relationships with others, especially our parents, should remain steadfast in our lives. If we think about the word "compromise", we often associate it with a positive action regarding our spouse or partner. We believe that we need to learn to compromise in order to have a healthy, mature, and stable relationship, without which, the marriage or partnership may break down. We feel so proud in telling others that we know how to compromise with our significant other. But, how often have we thought about the exact same thing with our parents? Do we joyfully tell our friends how mature we are, and that we have a great relationship with our parents because we know how to compromise with them? Is it only important and imperative to keep our marriage stable and happy? Should we only treat our spouse this way and not others, especially those who have been near and dear to us and brought us into this world?

No matter how responsible we may believe we are, our concept of independence being the definition of maturity is grounded in flawed reasoning. Genuine maturity involves *interdependence*, rather than *independence*. What are the differences between these two words, regarding our thoughts and actions? Independence is basically thinking, deciding, and acting alone, without assistance or guidance from others. Interdependence is when two or more people depend on each other, which in our context includes compromise, asking for advice and guidance, and having compassionate love and concern for each other, especially our parents and other caregivers. Interdependence is not the same as co-dependence, where a person relies on another person(s) for their needs and wants.

When we reach adulthood and are no longer dependent on our parents for our basic needs, we should be at a stage where we can willingly share thoughts, ideas, and parts of our lives with them. We ought to have a loving and comfortable, yet respectful relationship with our parents and enjoy spending time together with them. If something arises where our parent may need our help, we should pitch in to assist. Oftentimes, we may do things for our partner or best friends, but not for our parents. This is clearly a sign of immaturity, as we are putting our popularity before our parent's needs. To avoid the impulse to be independent, we need to think about how being interdependent is a much better way to act. Interdependence can build a stronger, healthier, happier, and more trusting relationship with our parents.

As our parents grow older, they will eventually need to be cared for. By applying the concept of interdependence with our spouse and our parents in our daily lives, it will be easier to undertake this responsibility without thinking it to be a burden. This will become indisputable once we understand that we all are children, even though we are grown up. Not losing sight of all that our parents have done to care for us, we can begin to appreciate that we are still their children and owe our gratitude to them.

~ ~ ~ ~ ~

Depending on our individual situation, there may be three types of parents in our life. They include:

1. Parents who gave us life. That is, our biological parents.
2. A parent or parents who raised us but are not our biological parents. This includes a parent/parents who adopted us either as an infant, or later in childhood.
3. A parent is also someone who has played a significant role in our upbringing with love and compassion. This may have included education, financial help, moral guidance, or emotional support. The person who has played such an important role in various parts of our life is by nature our parent even though that person did not give birth to us, nor raised us like our biological parents. This person may not even be a blood relative of ours.

Our biological parents have typically played the part of all three types of parents. They gave birth to us and loved and cared for us in many ways. They steered us in the right direction until we were ready to move into adulthood and face the challenges of our complex world. Parents who are not our biological parents but raised us in lieu of our birth parents are no different than our genetic parents. For instance, the Indian Prince Siddhartha's mother died only seven days after giving birth to him. His mother's younger sister then married his father for the sake of the baby prince. She raised him with unconditional love, compassion, and affection, just as his birth mother would have done. A clergy person or someone very close to us at a point in our lives when we were away from our birth parents, perhaps at school, are examples of the third type of parent. They may have played a significant role in our upbringing, education, moral guidance, or offering suggestions on our future goals. If we had the third type of parent, we are especially fortunate, as they spent their time and energy helping us out of genuine love and compassion, with a sense of deep concern for our well-being. They made sure that we were safe and secure, and often guided us with real challenges and uncertainties we may have faced in the world. In some ways, they are very special parents, as they had no obligation to care for us as much as our biological or adoptive parents did.

We rarely, if ever, think about what our parents have done for us, or how much they have loved and cared for us. We often feel that the "love of our life", whom we searched for on an Internet dating site or found at a bar is the person we should care about the most. But regardless of who we found, there is and will never be kinder and more compassionate people in our lives than our mother and father. Of course, we may find an enduring love relationship that may last a lifetime. But, as with any romantic relationship, there are strings attached. And at any moment, these strings can be broken forever. The love between parents and children is a different kind of love, as the love itself is enduring and has no strings attached. Therefore, our parents are worthy of our deep respect and trust beyond any reasonable doubt for their entire lifetime. It is impossible to repay our parents' acts of kindness, but as their children we should make every effort to fulfill our moral responsibilities towards them. These moral duties include maintaining a stable and healthy parent-child natural relationship and treating our parents with deep respect, humility, and serving them when they are in need of our help and support. We need to be mindful and understand that our parents' good health, both physically and emotionally, is our *real wealth*, and our parents' long life is our *genuine fortune*. Our parents' happiness should be our ultimate source of joy and blessings, but only if we allow this to happen. Adult children can never be virtuous and happy children if we do not keep these principles in our moral hearts and make sure to fulfill our moral responsibilities.

There are numerous moral responsibilities that ought to be fulfilled in order for parents and children to be happy in the natural parent-child relationship. They include, but are not limited to the following:

- Adult children should take a few minutes each day to refresh their awareness of their parent's kindness and make sure to be humble and respectful towards them.
- Make sure to check whether your parents are doing well and think about what you can do to help them if they need assistance.
- Live with a willingness to serve your parents when they need help and support, and especially when they become older.
- Try to be with your parents when they are lonely, sick, or unable to do things for themselves.
- Always thoughtfully consider your parent's words, advice, suggestions, and opinions instead of disregarding, ignoring, or disputing them. Children and adult children who go against their parent's kind and thoughtful words may not succeed or do very well in their lives.
- Never think that you are an adult and therefore may act towards your parents as you choose, or to treat them like your friends. Regardless of your age, you are always going to be a child in the face of your parents. Parents are not like friends in terms of their kindness to us. No friend can measure up to our parents, no matter how much we may like them.
- In day-to-day interactions with your parents, be diligent and try to use gentle words, have pleasant manners, talk less and listen more, think about how you can make your parents more comfortable, and make sure their needs are met. In

this way, your parents will be better able to lead a happy and healthy life.

- When gathering for family meals, holidays, dining out, or other occasions, always remember to serve your parents first. This simple form of humbleness is a sign of deep respect for parents, or for anyone else.

- Do not hide or conceal things from your parents. When you are confronted with difficult life situations, it is better to turn to them for guidance. They know you the best and are more able to help you than friends or strangers. Be sure to explain the situation in a considerate and thoughtful manner, so as not to worry your parents, which could lead to deeper problems. Hiding and concealing things from parents can lead to distrust, exclusion, and distancing from them.

- Adult children should always think about how the debt we owe to our parents is impossible to repay in our lifetime. However, adult children can and should attempt to compensate the debt of kindness through respect, humility, kindness, generosity, holding parents in high regard, wishing them to be happy, and serving and supporting them when they need help, particularly when they become old and unable to do things for themselves.

- Adult children should also be educated with a worthy skill and be reasonably successful and financially sound, so as not to be a burden or cause parents to worry.

All children, regardless of their age, should give serious thought to the following traditional Tibetan poem and vow to make a moral decision never to do such things to one's parents at any time in their lives.

Those (children) in whom I took delight,
For whose (children) existence I had longed,
They now are together with their wives,
Rejecting me (parent) as one would a hog.

Just as a worn-out horse is forced,
Away from food and driven from his shelter,
So too these children drive away their parents,
To beg for alms at other people's doors.

Just as a mule is used in work,
For years and years until worn out,
Then abandoned alone barely able to find food,
So too children of mine left me at the depressing nursing home.

As adult children, we should plan to do everything necessary to take good care of our parents when they become old. Most importantly, avoid consigning them to a nursing home, which can be very depressing and lonely for fragile, elderly people. One exception is if and when a parent reaches the stage where their condition warrants a hospice type of care. Adult children need to be aware that nursing homes and other professional care facilities are businesses that generally operate to make a profit. The services they provide cannot be given with the same love, compassion, and genuine concern that a child could give to his or her parent. If an elderly parent is eventually placed in a care facility, that does not mean that the children are "off the hook" with their moral responsibilities. In such cases, children and other family members should visit the elderly parent or relative often and call them on the phone frequently. Taking home-cooked food for lunch or dinner is beneficial. Sitting beside your parent, talking with them, and holding their hand can help with their emotional, psychological, and physical well-being. Remember that nursing home employees are not in the position to offer this type of care to your beloved parents.

We should reflect on how our parents, perhaps currently in good health, will eventually become old and frail. Elderly parents become somewhat like infants, needing care, support, nourishment, and love. We would not be here today — strong, healthy, educated, and successful — if our parents had abandoned us as infants, when we were fragile, vulnerable, and wholly unable to take care of ourselves. We adult children are obligated, both on moral grounds and human decency, to take care of our parents when they become old, sick, weak and in need of support, care, love, and physical and mental comfort.

There are several things to consider if parents choose to live in a nursing home or assisted living facility. First, try to make sure that they truly are making this choice without pressure or stress from others, social norms, or feelings of guilt. If the elderly see that "everyone" is moving to a nursing home, they may feel that they need to follow along, regardless of their true feelings. Also, elderly parents may feel guilty about having their children take care of them and not wanting to be a burden to the family. In reality, grandparents can complete the "family circle" and create a true to life learning environment for the entire family. Grandchildren can see firsthand how humans change as they grow older, what care they may need, and how to provide it. This can set the model for how children should take care of their parents when the time comes. Grandparents can provide a wealth of information for the entire family, by learning about how things were when they were young. This can lead to many interesting conversations and thoughts about how things in the past may not be old fashioned or needing to change or be discarded. Grandchildren and their grandparents can engage in fun activities, such as playing board games, reading books, learning crafts such as knitting or woodworking, and telling stories about their lives as children.

If indeed, parents do decide to move to a nursing home, adult children should agree and allow them to live as they choose. Make sure that the place they are moving to is safe, secure, and clean, has wholesome food, and activities for the residents. Also, check on the reputation of the nursing home to see if they are a certified caregiving facility. Sometimes elderly people do not want to complain, which can lead to discomfort or unhappiness. Therefore, from time to time, ask if everything is ok, or if they would like you to talk to the staff about any particular issues that need to be addressed. If your parents are physically able, take them to places away from the nursing home at least once a week, if possible. This may include going out for lunch or dinner, or taking outings to a park, museum, a movie, or the library. Also, visit them frequently and stay with them to chat, tell jokes, talk about important matters, and just to relax and be with them. This will help to brighten their minds and soothe their hearts.

Adults should never think that their old and fragile parents are in a nursing home "waiting for God". Make sure that they are living there because of the need for special assistance due to their age or health problems. Always continue to be dependable by providing them with all of the help and support that they may need. In reality, no one can predict who is on the verge of "meeting God" — a young and healthy child or an old and fragile person. It is totally unknown, unpredictable, and unfixed. Neither science nor astrology nor divination can correctly predict the exact time of death. It is important to bear this in mind and be humble, loyal, respectful, and eager to be there when our old parents are in need of help and support.

This poem can help us to not lose sight of all our parents have done for us:

For whom I've given painful births,
Have raised them with love and care,
Now I become old and in need of their support,
But in the place of support they've left me alone like trash.
It is the saddest thing in my life.

Just as a mother hen keeps her chicks in the nest,
Providing all the safety and protection.
Fed and helped them build the strength of their wings,
And sent them into the real world with all the means to take care of
themselves.
I too have done similar for my children, but at the end,
I am left alone being ill, weak, old, and in darkness and loneliness.

I raised my children with love,
But they returned my love with disobedience.
I taught them good and gave them moral guidance,
But they returned my goodness with rebellion.

This poem embodies the emotions and ruminations that elderly parents may experience when forsaken by their adult children. If their offspring do not have a natural feeling of love and respect for their parents, they become void of kindness and humility. This indicates a form of rebellion. Regardless of the situation, an adult child should never rebel against his or her parents. Rebelling against one's parents is an extremely immoral behavior and can be more harmful to their parents' well-being than any other ill deeds.

No one should ever allow their parents to be exposed to this type of situation, even from siblings. Harbor them from negative and harmful experiences by carefully monitoring how they are being treated. Moreover, children and adult children should always call their parents mother or father, or mom or dad. Calling a parent by their given name is wholly disrespectful and arrogant. One is never at the same level as one's parents, regardless of their age.

I introduced my children to the world with good manners,
But they turned into immoral and disgraceful adults.
It has injured my heart and caused it to bleed with pain.
What have I done wrong to have such ungrateful children?

I gave painful births to my children,
I took delight at their births.
I cherished them as being more important than my own life,
At the end, I was treated as any other person by my own children.

Adult children need to be mindful not to create unnecessary problems, heartache, or moral dilemmas for their parents. Never do anything that would allow a parent to think that it would be better to have no children than to have ungrateful ones. This stanza clearly conveys the anguish and grief from the loss of a child through estrangement:

Better a stick, I say, would be,
Than ungrateful children estranging me.
At least it can be used as a walking cane,
Or to drive away a parish dog.

Repaying our parents' kindness does not mean providing them with money or other material gifts. It means giving them love, care, compassion, and attention, which fulfills children's moral responsibilities to their parents. However, giving material help to parents may be necessary when parents are old, suffering from an illness, or not having adequate means to support themselves.

In general, children's moral responsibilities owed to their parents have no limitations. However, the following are some of the most important responsibilities that are possible in the modern world. Adult children should keep a mental list of these vows to live by. They should be remembered like the words carved in a loved one's memorial stone.

1. I shall support my parents since they once supported me.
2. I shall take on the duties incumbent on me to my parents.
3. I shall listen carefully to their words, follow them faithfully, and practice moral values.
4. I shall not misuse their material gifts.
5. I shall never lie to my parents and will always be truthful and speak gently to them.
6. I shall never be arrogant to my parents and shall place myself at the lowest level in their presence.
7. I shall never be biased against my parents or treat them differently.
8. I shall always go to them whenever they need my help.
9. I shall always maintain a healthy relationship with my parents.

10. I shall never speak slander to or against my parents.
11. I shall always revere my parents with respect and humility.
12. I shall please my parents through good actions, deeds, and words.
13. I shall always place my parents' needs at the top of my agenda.
14. I shall never let my parents down by doing immoral actions.
15. I shall make my parents feel proud of me by being upright and successful.
16. I shall always say prayers for my parents' good health and longevity.
17. I shall devote myself to serving my parents since they devoted their lives to raising me and guiding me to where I now stand — strong, healthy, educated, in an environment conducive to healthy and comfortable living.
18. I shall never forget my parents' struggles to guide me in the right direction in my life, enabling me to stand on my own to make me a good and happy person.

An adult child's role in fulfilling their moral duty is not to pay their parents back. Parents are not waiting in anticipation to harvest their crop and reap the benefits for all they have done for their children. The child's moral duty is simply that, a responsibility with no strings attached. Nevertheless, there can be many negative consequences resulting from adult children (and all children) not fulfilling their moral responsibilities towards their parents. Adult children who do not listen, reflect on, nor pay heed to their parents' advice can lead to negative consequences in the future. They may face many struggles, challenges, hardships, and obstacles in pursuit of success and happiness. Many times, as teenagers and young adults, we are enticed into believing what society, politicians, or activists say will make us happy or fulfill our wants, desires, aspirations, and needs. We often disregard our wise parents, while being lured by others. We may falsely believe that because we are intelligent and well educated, we cannot be misled by promises or incorrect information. When this happens, we need to stop and reflect on what we are being told and discuss these ideas with our parents. They may be able to encourage us to think more deeply about these matters and perhaps come to a different conclusion.

Similarly, when children or adult children lie to their parents, this can lead to very negative outcomes. Once a person lies to his or her parents, they tend to continue lying and become a very bad liar indeed. Lying to one's parents opens himself or herself up to becoming a liar in society, which can lead to lying without hesitation or having a moral sense of respect and self-dignity. Children of all ages who lie to their parents can suffer the worst moral downfall on the basis of the sacred natural relationship between parents and their children. Children, and especially adult children, should know that there is no pain more severe than the pain of children openly lying to their parents. Always make sure never to lie to your parents about anything by making a conscious moral decision to always be truthful to them. To emphasize this in more detail, it is not acceptable to lie to your parents and later disclose the truth. That is still telling a lie, and later telling the truth is not an excuse or pardonable for lying in the first place.

While actions such as not listening to a parent's advice or lying to them can have serious consequences, the egregious act of neglecting a parent who faces a health or monetary crisis is of greatest concern. Failure to support or help a parent who is in need will certainly lead to negative and harmful repercussions, most significantly for the suffering parent. Not coming to their aid can harm the parent's physical and emotional health, as well as their comfort and safety. Negative consequences for the adult child may include a rapid degeneration of their wealth, health, reputation, social status, and friendships in the latter part of their life. An example of this was a woman who neglected her mother who was undergoing an eight-hour hip replacement surgery. The mother, who was in severe pain, called her daughter for help during the evening. The daughter's response was that she could not come because she was going to a party at a friend's house. For her, going to a party was more important than going to help her ailing mother who was unable to take care of herself. The daughter's immoral behavior towards her kind mother led to many negative consequences: a bitter divorce, loneliness, joblessness, psychological problems, and a loss of trust and respect. Nevertheless, even if the daughter's actions had no negative results to herself, the mother did suffer, and that is what matters the most.

In many Eastern cultures, parents have traditionally been treated by their children in a godlike manner, or at least as worthy of trust, respect, and a source of wise advice and a path of good conduct. Breaking the natural parent-child relationship in these cultures has widely been considered to be highly negative by nature, and not just on social grounds. It is understood that this relationship must be well maintained with deep respect for the best and highest mutual interest of parents and their children. This sacred parent-child relationship has been shown over the centuries to develop into a cohesive, loving family, which has brought lasting joy and riches to the family unit.

Many in the West or other "developed" countries may see some of these ideas as archaic, obsolete, and perhaps illogical; being out of touch with the reality of the contemporary world. Today's modern children often call their parents and teachers by their first names, even in elementary school. Parents may proclaim that their children are their best friends. TV commercials portray parents as being ignorant and their children as being wise. These may seem like insignificant things with no negative consequences. But if children treat their parents as equals, and even give advice to their parents, how can children truly develop into responsible, insightful, and compassionate adults who respect their parents' wisdom and guidance? Contrarily, many teenagers and young adults seem to be wandering about, lost in a world with less and less interaction with their parents. Some have grown up to become lonely and dissatisfied, instead of content and connected to family and society. As adults, they have lost the ability to understand the need for and goodness in having a close-knit nuclear family. They have become consumed with their own life, with their parents being long forgotten.

If one looks deeply into the "eyes" of modern society, one does not often see a sparkle, but a profound, hollow emptiness. We have lost a stability in our world that is so essential for humans to thrive and grow in a wholesome way. When there is no sparkle, you can clearly see that our young people are blindly following society's ways. We must bring the sparkle back in order to light up our children's aspirations. This needs to be the goal of modern society. Our children can then grow up to be the happy, kind, and ethical adult children we will all admire.

CHAPTER 6

Ethical Guidance for Adults and Children

UNDERSTANDING WHAT CONSTITUTES ethical be-
havior, and how each of us should employ ethical principles
in our lives is extremely important. For society to thrive or
even survive in a decent way, learning and adhering to ethical
standards is crucial. Some may believe that we are very advanced in
our thinking and way of living, as we have more formal education,
know more about the world, and are savvy about things such as
technical devices. Our forbearers generally had far less formal education, knew little about the outside world, and were unfamiliar with
scientific theories, modern medical treatments, and other things we
take for granted nowadays. This being said, perhaps we need to ask
ourselves some pertinent questions about ethics:

- Have we comprehensively studied ethics in a formal setting?
- Do we think about our ethical behavior on a regular basis?
- Will our children grow up to be ethical individuals, both in
  their personal and working lives?
- If we believe so, what have we done to help ensure that this
  will happen?

To help our children learn about ethics and similar subjects such as values and morals, we must first become knowledgeable about these topics ourselves. Each and every day we make ethical decisions — primarily without even recognizing it. Some ethical situations we may be confronted with include medical, financial, and legal matters. In broader terms, ethics may include being honest, fair, trustworthy, law-abiding, having concern for others, and respecting different viewpoints. Before we can help our children learn about ethics, we need to carefully examine how we have made choices regarding ethical dilemmas we have faced. Were our decisions based on personal wants or needs, or because we genuinely considered the ethical thing to do in each case? A good starting point in thinking and behaving in an ethical way is to deem all people as being equal and as important as oneself, while attempting to treat everyone with fairness and benevolence. It also means allowing others to have their own points of view on religion, social matters, politics, and personal choices.

No one is perfect, and we will all make decisions and act in ways that may not have been the best choice. Nevertheless, we should strive to lead a good life and cause no harm. If we truly feel free from guilt, blame, or shame by not doing anything deleterious, illegal, or harmful to oneself or others, we most likely are being ethical. Negative actions can make our lives impure, with a disturbing sense of being somber and contaminated. These feelings can be immensely detrimental to our well-being and can inhibit us from becoming a better and happier person. Leading an ethical life is extremely important to be composed and serene, full of confidence and inner strength. An ethical life is a wholesome life, worthy of trust, respect, admiration, and inspiration. A life without ethics can become a life filled with adversity and hardships, regardless of whether we are highly educated or wealthy.

In many cases, we may believe that other factors — a bad boss, a low salary, or an unsupportive spouse or parent is the cause of our problems. If we have built up a large debt, we may attribute it to credit card companies. If we smoke cigarettes, we may blame the cigarette manufacturers or advertisers. Instead of faulting others, we need to look at our own behaviors, which in all likelihood are the cause of many of our troubles. We truly need to understand that most of the problems we face come from unethical conduct of what we do, say, and think, brought about by the influences of a spoiled mind. Leading an ethical life can assuredly solve many of the problems that we encounter, while preventing suffering to ourselves and others.

Before going further, we need to recognize the distinction between religious views of ethics and the type of ethics referred to in this book. Here, ethics comprises the difference between good versus bad, positive versus negative, and beneficial versus harmful in the natural world. For example, *stealing* is universally accepted as being bad, negative, and harmful irrespective of religious faith or teachings. *Generosity* is universally considered as good, positive, and beneficial. The widespread belief that stealing is bad and generosity is good has nothing to do with religious teachings or beliefs. Stealing is by its nature bad and negative. Generosity is by its nature good and positive. Therefore, ethics in this context connotes helping children to develop and exercise self-discipline to avoid actions that are negative by their nature, while cultivating actions that are positive.

It is especially important to guard children against forming these types of behaviors, as young ones are not even aware of the damage or ramifications they may hold in adulthood. The unavoidable natural consequences of unethical behavior can last a lifetime. These behaviors may be avoidable if parents can guide and correct their children starting at a young age. At an early age, children should be shown by example the expected natural consequences of their actions, rather than telling them: *Do this as it is good.* or *Don't do that as it is bad.* In contrast, parents, teachers, or other adults should explain to the child: *You may cut yourself if you pick up that knife. Do you want that to happen?* Most likely, the child may reply by saying: *No, mom (or dad). I do not want that to happen to me.* It can be helpful for parents or teachers to restate the question by asking: *Are you sure?* If the child replies without hesitation, then he or she certainly understands the meaning of what you are explaining. Youngsters have a natural inclination to be either ethical or unethical, and it is very important for parents and teachers to notice these tendencies and help guide children to be more ethical, considerate, and stable. Parents can begin by teaching their young children the differences between good and bad through stories and fables. By using an animated voice and facial expressions, small children are more apt to pay close attention and become involved in the story. It is important to make certain that children understand the message conveyed in the tale, as grasping the subject matter can help children comprehend the implications of the actions narrated in the story.

To help foster a deep and abiding ethical life, young children need to be taught about certain universal ethical mores, including lying, killing, and stealing. This should be done gently and consistently throughout their childhood to form a concrete understanding of right and wrong. Lying can lead to many difficult situations throughout a person's lifetime, and even "white lies" can cause harm to the perpetrator and others. It is not enough to simply tell a child not to lie. Have discussions about what constitutes a lie, as lies are far more complex than telling a falsehood. Many people feel that it is a harmless action to kill bugs and certain animals. Children may see parents, playmates, and others openly kill living creatures, especially insects. Witnessing these acts can leave an impression on the innocent child that killing is normal or okay, depending on what is being killed. One needs to seriously consider the effects of exposing children to such actions. Parents need to explain to their children that stealing is not just robbing a bank, taking merchandise from a store, or money from someone's pocket. For children, stealing may include taking candy from a bowl on the table or an answer on another child's homework assignment. Children must understand that stealing something, anything, from another person or place is not borrowing it, as that requires asking permission, with the intent to return the borrowed item. By asking children simple, straightforward questions, such as *Do you want others to treat you as a liar?* (or killer, thief, cheater) you sow the seeds for the child to think about his or her actions and their potential outcomes. Explaining these actions and their possible consequences can help a child to think in advance about doing wrong. A parent might say: *Do you want to hurt an innocent bug, or take something that belongs to someone else? I don't think so. You are a good child and I want you to become an even better person. This type of behavior may make you very unhappy, and your friends may not like you anymore. Or, your teacher may think you are not trustworthy. That will certainly make you very unhappy.* By showing children the negative consequences of bad actions and rewarding the results of good actions, the child will begin to see that one is one's own rewarder and one's own punisher, instead of someone else. This is an extremely valuable lesson to learn, as it carries into adulthood. This way, children can understand that saying: *The dog ate my homework.* is not a reasonable or responsible answer for not doing the homework.

Teaching children right from wrong is not only important for not getting into trouble and being well behaved. More importantly, it is a parent's moral duty to make clear to their children the possible outcomes of their actions before sending them into a world filled with so many negative forces and influences. Even decent children may easily become lost in this troubled and turbulent world, like Nemo getting lost in the vast ocean, suffering from being caught and kept in a small tank with unsavory fish. These problems happened to Nemo because he did not listen to his kind and concerned parents. Nemo wanted to do things his way. His behavior led him to undergo many unexpected problems in the vast, unknown ocean, rife with many dangerous species. This movie plot is akin to the enormous number of negative forces and bad influences humans encounter in our world. Once children become adults, they may suffer greatly if they have not listened to their parents' moral guidance and wisdom.

As stated above, the ethics described in this book is a secular, temporal way of behaving and understanding what is right and wrong. It is not a religious concept or moral creed. Rather, it is a way of doing good actions and staying away from bad and harmful thoughts and actions in everyday life. This type of behavior can help to shape society into a better place for everyone to live and thrive.

~ ~ ~ ~ ~

There are three stages of ethics that can be integrated into daily life and blend well with formal education. Adults, and especially parents and teachers, who are reasonably knowledgeable and follow these ethical principles, will be better able to guide children to grow and thrive with an ethical mindset.

The three ethical stages for adults to fully understand and practice include:

Ethics of restraint

This pertains to ensuring that we abandon actions that are harmful to ourselves and all other beings. *"Restraint"* means staying away from something or someone through our deliberate conscious effort. It means to avoid *obviously harmful actions and behaviors* for the best and greatest interest of everyone, including ourselves.

Ethics of doing beneficial deeds

This relates to working for the sake of others, including the elderly, disabled persons, anyone who needs help, and animals. It includes working for the interest of the community and society as a whole to support, protect, and offer comfort, assistance, and aid to others.

Ethics of altruistic endeavors

This concerns compassion, kindness, unselfishness, and self-sacrifice for the well-being of all others, regardless of any past negative thoughts or actions towards us. Without harboring ill will, revenge, or holding negative thoughts, do whatever it requires to be of service to anyone who is in need of help.

While all three stages of ethics are very important, we will focus on the **ethics of restraint** in this book. In general, there are countless harmful actions and behaviors. The following are examples of some of the most harmful actions, all of which need to be avoided or unconditionally abandoned.

Do not murder (meaning the willful killing of any human being, for any reason)

If you commit murder once you become a murderer. You will always be treated as a murderer and this cannot be washed away until you die. Having committed murder one time in your lifetime is akin to having a permanent tattoo that will never disappear until your body is cremated. Committing a murder is extremely negative and wholeheartedly harmful for the peace and well-being of society. Always make sure to live with a strong and firm commitment never to commit murder, regardless of the situation you find yourself in. If possible, recite this once a day upon awaking in the morning to absolutely stay away from committing murder:

I shall never commit murder for any reason in my entire life for the greatest well-being of everyone.

I shall maintain my life as wholesome, blameless, shameless, and guiltless.

I shall respect all forms of life and live with a moral dignity that brings me courage and self-confidence.

Do not steal

If you steal once in your life you become a thief. You will always be treated as a thief and this can never be erased until you die. You may steal out of habit, you may steal because you need something, you may steal due to jealousy, you may steal because of covetousness, and you may steal because you want to do harm for false gratification.

Many unethical behaviors have their roots in the mind. Therefore, you must be observant and aware of your mind and your thoughts. Make sure to shatter negative and harmful thoughts as soon as they arise. Just hammer them away; do not allow them to control you. In the case of stealing for needs, then begging is much better than stealing, as there is nothing morally wrong with begging. Getting what you need through stealing is by nature negative and the stolen object cannot be very helpful for your life and needs. One caveat — you must make certain that you truly need what you are begging for and are not begging simply because you do not want to solve a problem by your own means. Never lie to yourself to get something you simply want and can do without. If indeed you find that you must beg, as there is no personal remedy for the situation, you will remain innocent and can lead your life in a wholesome way with no negative consequences of blame, shame, guilt, or fear.

Do not lie or cheat

No one should lie, and in our context, particularly parents, teachers, and children's caregivers. If an adult lies to a child, the child may not know or understand that what was said was an untruth. The child may become confused and upset, especially if he or she later discovers the truth. Therefore, do not tell a falsehood to anyone, including children. Lying is by nature negative, which will certainly have adverse consequences in your own life and will do harm to others. The plain and simple truth is that if you lie, you will be a liar for the rest of your life. You will be treated as a liar by society and you will have a difficult time succeeding in your endeavors and finding happiness. So as not to misunderstand, lying means intentionally telling an untruth or making false statements for either personal gain by deceiving others or a wish to deliver harm to others based on a personal dislike of the person or for revenge. Lying is one of the worst forms of false speech and will inevitably lead to detrimental consequences that cannot be avoided. Be aware that lies leak into the mainstream sooner or later, as there is no moral basis of truth in a lie. With candor and genuineness, the truth will always remain true and will never leak.

It is easy for behaviors to turn into habits, either good or bad. Consequently, it is important for parents and caregivers to teach children, beginning at a young age, to form the habit of telling the truth. This needs to be taught and explained repeatedly in order for children to be aware of how to be honest in various situations, and the positive outcomes of this behavior. Part of the teaching for developing the habit of truthfulness should include the ultimate *goodness* in telling the truth and the eventual negativities and despair of lying. The ensuing negative consequences of lying can always be avoided, which is critical for children to comprehend. Without fully understanding the consequences of lying, children may wander from the path of truthfulness to the byway of deceit. Parents should never take truth telling for granted; it needs to be taught and reinforced with kindness and sincerity. You should cheer with joy when your child is truthful, just as you would cheer with glee when your child wins a race. A good message for adults to contemplate is that the formed habit of telling the truth is primarily dependent on the habit of thinking correctly and clearly in an attempt to relate whatever the narrative, account, or description may be. Telling a lie requires thinking, planning and scheming. Therefore, during this process there is always time to stop and reflect on what is happening and change the thought process to bring about a positive and honest conclusion.

Cheating is a form of lying, with a different nuance. Lies are generally verbal mistruths, while cheating is an action that a person engages in. Cheating typically involves games (cheating at cards), sports, on examinations, or on a spouse or partner. When someone purposely breaks the rules, they are cheating. Specific rules are usually stated for games or sports, and should not be broken. Cheating on an exam may involve looking at another student's paper, copying information that is not the student's own writing, or using a "cheat sheet" to look at during an exam. Cheating on a spouse or partner engages a third person in being unfaithful. This type of cheating truly betrays the trust of the spouse. Cheating is generally a sneaky, devious action that is meant to trick, dupe, or double-cross another person. It is not unusual for cheaters to "get away" with their deceit, as they may never be caught by the victim. Cheating is very harmful and hurtful, and highly unethical. Therefore, one should never engage in any form of cheating. Parents need to explain what cheating is, even while playing a simple game. This negative undertaking must be addressed and corrected when it happens, so as not to form a very harmful habit.

Do not spread rumors

Rumors are similar to lies, as they are declarations or pronouncements that are based on speculation or hearsay. When someone relates a rumor to another person, it tends to spread and multiply, as a fire spreads and grows bigger. Many people seem to feel excited and fascinated by telling and listening to rumors and gossip. But they need to be aware that rumors are very harmful and damaging to the victim's name, reputation, and social status. By circulating rumors, you will become a rumor maker and your words will not be treated with respect. As a result, your words will have very little positive impact on others.

One of the best ways to avoid creating rumors is to stay away from indulging in idle chit-chat or idle gossip. Idle gossip creates all kinds of confusion and unfortunate misunderstandings, which can lead people to become enemies by undermining trust and creating hurtful feelings. Telling and listening to rumors and gossip is also a waste of precious time and energy. There are so many good and necessary things to do with the limited amount of time we have each day away from work and sleep. Sitting around simply chit-chatting is laziness, as it accomplishes nothing. If you are lazy, you will not be in a position to do the things that need to be done today. You cannot do any good if you procrastinate and are fond of idleness. This can lead to boredom, which is often when rumors and gossip originate.

Do not adopt wrong livelihood

Wrong livelihood is connected to many negative actions of the body, speech, and mind. These sources of income or sustenance are by their nature harmful to others as well as to yourself. By choosing a way to accumulate money or other objects with the sole purpose of procuring needs or wants can certainly lead to a wrong approach in determining your livelihood. Wrong livelihood includes more than a certain type of job. It encompasses such things as trying to gain material benefits from others through pretense, using attractive words to gain things from others through deceit, praising another's possessions with the intention of trying to obtain them for yourself, forcibly taking what belongs to someone else, and extolling the qualities of what one has obtained in the past with the hope of getting more in the future.

Wrong livelihood also includes dealing with weapons, alcoholic beverages, illegal drugs, poisons, brothels, butchers*, human-trafficking, production of toxic chemicals that create contamination in the environment, and many other detrimental aspects of making a living. By being exposed to the negative factors involved in these areas, many seen and unseen adverse occurrences may happen to you and to others. Adoption of a wholesome livelihood is far better for you and all others.

*Please note that in this context, the term "butcher" means one whose occupation is slaughtering animals for meat, hide, or fur. In the Tibetan language, the term shenpa means a person who kills animals. In English, "butcher" can have dual meanings; one who slaughters animals or one who prepares the meat for sale or is a meat merchant. The second meaning is not considered as a wrong livelihood.

The above types of wrong livelihood are rather easy to understand. However, one also needs to consider the moral and ethical aspects of individual employment situations. If an employer or company is knowingly doing wrong, working in that particular situation could also be considered as wrong livelihood. Examples of these types of circumstances may include observing illegal practices such as tax evasion, embezzlement, discrimination, producing faulty products, or other means of wrongdoing. In these types of cases, if a solution cannot be found, it may be better to find new employment rather than ignoring the situation.

Do not use drugs or drink an excessive amount of alcohol

Many of humankind's problems involve cravings; cravings for just about anything — perhaps a new car, warm and sunny weather, chocolate, coffee, shopping for new clothes, or surfing the Internet. While cravings seem to be normal and controllable, some can often lead to grave health and life issues. That extra cup of coffee or a daily candy bar may not lead to worrying health concerns or financial ruin, but drugs and excessive use of alcohol need to be thought of differently. Drugs, including over-the-counter medicines, cigarettes and marijuana, as well as alcoholic beverages, can ruin the lives of you and your family, as these cravings often lead to addictions, which are very difficult to control. People may make excuses or justifications for using addictive and harmful substances. They may place the blame on other things — parents, genetics, corporations, advertisements, friends, social pressures, or stress. Many of these may behaviors may become habits that are formed during school years, sometimes as early as elementary school. It certainly may be difficult for a young person to understand the ramifications drugs or alcohol can have on the mind and body. They are simply following their friends, wanting to be liked and have a good time. This is why it is urgent for parents to educate their children, starting in elementary school, about the hazards of engaging in these types of behavior.

It is interesting to watch an animal, say a pet cat, to see how they react to unhealthy or bad food. They take one whiff of the food, and if it is not safe smelling, they immediately back away and refuse to eat it. Humans are not that intuitive or intelligent when it comes to what we put in our mouths. Even if we dislike the substance, we often keep trying it until we learn to accept it as good. Could we honestly say that a cigarette, beer or whisky tasted good the first time we tried them? Most likely not. This is something worth discussing with your pre-teens and teenagers.

To gain awareness of our cravings, be they ever so subtle, it may be helpful to consider why harmful substances create desires, which may turn into urges and addictions. These include:

- Alcohol — do you drink to socialize, to be popular and fit in, or to reduce stress?
- Cigarettes — do you smoke to rebel, or to feel it is a personal right?
- Drugs — do you take over-the-counter pain relievers as soon as you have an ache, or do you desire illegal drugs to get "high"?
- Marijuana — now that it is legal in several states, is this a justification to use it?

By analyzing these substances, we may start to discover the true cause of our wanting to engage in using any of these harmful things. We may begin to understand the lack of any positive outcomes and see some negative results. All of them cost money, they can harm our physical health and mental well-being, they can lead to dependencies, and they can cause relationships to suffer with our family and friends. If we feel that we are free and independent to choose to take these drugs, have we thought about what happens when we cannot quit or do without them? Rather than being independent, the drugs can make us dependent on them. It therefore follows that it makes no sense to give up our family, friends, job, or health for any of these harmful habits. If you do ignore all of the warning signs, at least do not allow yourself to be in denial of the possible consequences. By rejecting the cautionary signals, it is more likely that you may fail to be prudent. That, in turn, could lead to becoming an alcoholic or a drug user, with an irreversible and irreparable habit of addiction. The outcome may ruin your health, dishevel your mind, squander your wealth, and destroy your relationships with loved ones.

Being an addict defeats the purpose of life, perhaps becoming an outcast from society. Life as an outcast is a very isolated place, filled with loneliness, depression, addiction, poverty, hunger, and deep misery. Never allow your own bad habits and lackadaisical attitudes to prevent you from living a good, upstanding life. You need to be very mindful of your thoughts and tendencies and be aware of the consequences of your disruptive and undisciplined actions. Always remember that taking drugs or drinking alcohol may temporarily numb your pain but will inevitably lead to bigger problems and more pain. There is an old saying: *Do not do anything that causes you to get a scar on your head that is bigger than your head itself.* The message here is — do not try to find a solution for a problem that causes you to have a bigger problem than the one you are attempting to solve. The best action is to never take comfort in drugs or alcohol as a remedy for your inner agony and pain.

Of course, it is fine to have a glass of wine with a healthy meal and part of a social gathering. But never drink more than a glass or two, as there is no good reason to do so. It is also reasonable to take pain medicine when necessary. However, never take more than is needed. If a doctor prescribes a pain medicine, question the doctor on what is the *least* amount of medicine needed. Indicate to the doctor that you do not want to take more than is absolutely necessary.

Do not engage in violent behavior

Violence seems to surround us in this modern world. We see violent acts and hear violence on the news, on TV shows and movies, in modern music and books, in neighborhoods and homes, and even while driving our cars. Terrorism and modern warfare predominate our life, with no reason or rationale for what is truly causing this to happen or how to stop or prevent these acts from occurring. Violence is generally considered a physical aggression that causes bodily or psychological harm. But the films, books, news, and music we are exposed to can also be considered as violence, as these can also do psychological harm. While we cannot find easy answers or solutions for the violence in our world, we can take steps to protect our families and ourselves from too much exposure to these forms of violence. Moreover, we can be more mindful to never think or act in ways that are violent in nature or show a lack of restraint.

More and more, our children are unprotected from seeing these forms of violence, and are susceptible to their influences. Adults, and especially parents and teachers, need to protect and educate our children about violent-type childhood behavior. When children are young, we need to be careful about how to handle such behaviors as stubbornness and temper tantrums. This type of conduct can become habituated and may lead to anger problems later in life. The more a child is educated in coping with emotions and actions, the better prepared they will be in facing difficult situations throughout their lives.

A few suggestions for handling temper tantrums and stubborn behavior include the following:

- Ignore the child's reactions if not too serious. They will see that their behavior is not getting them the attention they seek.
- Keep calm, even if your child is screaming or kicking.
- Never yell or get angry, but do not let your child think that throwing a temper tantrum is acceptable.
- Firmly and calmly tell him that his actions are not ok. Tell him that kicking can hurt the person, and yelling is upsetting to others.
- Sit down with your child and gently tell her to take a deep breath to calm down. You can do the same to model this action.
- Tell her you are going to talk with her about the situation. She will begin to learn that talking is better than yelling. (Note: this does not mean that the child can negotiate to get what she wants or demands.)
- Make sure that your child is rested and not hungry before going shopping, to a playground, or other outings.

It is also important to teach children to care — about themselves, the family pet, grandparents, siblings, and even insects. A child who is shown how to release a bug to the outside world without killing it will certainly learn to understand the concept of doing no harm to any living being. A home environment where all beings are treated with kindness, helpfulness, and thoughtfulness will create a warm and loving atmosphere for all. Do not watch violent TV shows or movies, and don't allow your children to watch them either. Regarding adults, avoid engaging in violent thoughts or feelings. Thinking in a non-violent way will naturally control your actions to become more peaceful and gentler. In Eastern philosophy, the concept of *Ahimsa,* which means *peace, non-aggression,* and *non-violence,* encompasses the spirit of non-violence. Patience, respect, proper discernment, self-confidence, and conviction using peaceful means to solve problems are indispensable qualities for adopting a non-violent life.

Do not be friends with those who behave badly and have contagious negative habits.

Having friends is an important and vital part of our lives. Humans are social beings and are not meant to live primarily alone. Nearly all of us had playmates as children — mostly from our neighborhoods and schools. These companions helped us to be happy and flourish. Just the same, adults thrive with friendships as well. With a few close and trusted friends, we can confide in them about problems, listen to suggestions, and simply spend time together over a nice meal, a long walk, or a vacation. Friends can help guide us in the right path, boost our energy, and learn something healthful or rewarding. We find solace in our friends in times of sorrow and laugh with them in times of joy. It is important to have at least one close friend throughout our life. However, it is not as easy to find a true friend in adulthood as when we were youngsters. We may have moved away from our hometown. Or, we may have had a very close friend who moved far away or who has died. These factors may lead to frustration in trying to find friendship at a later stage in life. Nevertheless, we should not rush to find a friend in order to cure our loneliness or provide help. It is wise to look for a potential friend who is moral, thoughtful, respectful, and kind.

Since it is often less difficult for children to form friendships, parents may not be overly concerned about who their children are playing with. When difficulties arise, it may be easy to say that kids will be kids. Learning how to make and keep long-lasting friends develops from childhood experiences, so this is the time for parents to educate their young ones on this subject. Parents need to play a watchful role by guiding their children in the right direction, and to be taught and shown the difference between good and bad friends. At the same time, parents need to make sure that "bad" children are not treated poorly or ostracized. Based on the different stages of childhood development, parents should determine what types of activities and behaviors their children should engage in with their friends.

In the Western world, the turning point for the family structure took place after the Great Depression (circa 1929 — mid-1930s). Before this time, the family generally consisted of adults — parents and grandparents — and children. There was no mid-point between the two categories. With the advent of motorized vehicles, school buses and automobiles came into use. This meant the end of the one-room schoolhouse. Along with this, young people were learning to drive the family car, which gave them the freedom to stray further away from home. Older children (the term "teenager" was not coined until the 1940s) began to be grouped together in consolidated schools with students of the same age. Parents had less control over the whereabouts of their offspring, and who they were associating with. Thus began the rise of a third group in the family structure — the teenager.

In earlier times, when children in their teen years were attached to their home and parents, they clearly were under much less influence from the outside world. In contemporary society, the teenage years are more problematic in many ways. Teens have become much more independent, with many having their own cars, jobs, and credit cards. At this crucial stage of development, new friendships and more intimate relationships are often formed. The desire to be popular may lead teens to choose unacceptable friends and engage in harmful activities.

What are parents to do? Nowadays, with the internet, online dating sites, and places where teenagers are exposed to drugs, alcohol, and other bad influences, it is simply not possible to know everything your teenagers are doing. The best advice is to begin to counsel and guide your children in the right direction from a very young age. Treat them with love, affection, care, and help give them advice in difficult situations they may encounter in their lives. Always be there for them. Let them know that you are, as their parent, responsible for leading them into the adult world, to be successful, happy, and a decent and moral person. Parents also need to keep a watchful eye on teens' whereabouts and activities. They may protest, saying that their friends are allowed to do such and such, but do not let their objections change your stance. While teenagers are growing into adulthood and need to develop more personal responsibilities, they should not be given free rein to do as they choose. Their friends should not be your friends, but they should not be strangers either. Have your teenager invite his or her friends to the house and from time to time go to a movie or a ball game together. This way, you will be able to better judge the friends' character.

Some words of caution to be noted:

- Parents, nor their children, should believe that they are best friends with each other. Friends are typically found among peer groups, and parents are parents. Be sure not to confuse the two.
- Friends are very important for all humans to have. That being said, friends can also betray you. They may tell others private things that you held in close confidence with them. Friends can try to coerce you to drink, experiment with drugs, and form triangular relationships out of jealousy. Never keep a dysfunctional friendship that may be based on

your desire not to be lonely. No friend is better than a bad friend.

- If you get into a serious love relationship, you should not cast aside your friends. This is harmful to everyone. One person — your new love interest — should not encompass your entire life. This can turn into a strong attachment where your vision and senses are clouded. Your long-term friends can advise and warn you about your behavior, if you are willing to listen and trust their advice.

- Nowadays, grown up children are prone to rely on their friends for advice more than their parents. Adult children do not realize that their new-found college friends do not know them well and do not have any insight into their family or cultural background. Young adults are wise to confide in the prudence of their parents and not rely on friends to help solve serious problems. If they were honest with themselves, they would understand that they may not be seeking advice from their friends, but rather looking for confirmation of what they want to do.

An ancient adage about life states:

May I never meet with bad friends.

May I never get caught in bad influences of others in the name of friendship.

May I be alone in goodness instead of in a circle of bad friends.

May I always be guided by the awareness of "having no friends is far better than having bad friends."

~ ~ ~ ~ ~

Habits *help shape our behavior.*

All of these actions can certainly be harmful and should be avoided or abandoned under all circumstances. It is easy to fall into thinking that it is okay to cheat, lie, or spread rumors once in a while, as long as it does not become a habit. But this is a trap, as once can turn into a few times, and then to many times. The habit becomes set in your behavior, without even thinking about the harm an action may bring to yourself or others. You may begin to believe that your formed habits are simply who you are; your nature, your predisposition, or propensity to act in certain ways. But that is not the case. A **habit** is a *developed* inclination that motivates you to repeat a particular action over and over again without requiring you to think about or plan to do the action. Habits such as drinking alcohol, using drugs, and gambling can certainly create problems in your life. Good habits can develop as well, such as healthy routines — eating nutritious foods, getting exercise, and getting enough sleep.

Drinking is a troubling problem among many people in the world, particularly where it is accepted or even promoted as part of the culture. This may influence people to think: *I need to be a part of the drinking culture, or I may not be welcome at social gatherings or events.* Unfortunately, it is the culture that motivates people to drink because the habit of drinking has become a part of the culture. Similarly, a drinking habit may become a part of your life and you may not be able to live without drinking. This habit may then lead to an addiction to alcohol.

Teenagers, and even pre-teens face many obstacles and temptations in society, as they are surrounded by peers who may pressure them to conform. It is imperative for parents to inform and educate their children of the dangers of drinking alcohol, including its illegality for underage drinking. Likewise, drinking and driving can lead to being arrested, losing a driver's license, injury to the self or others, or even worse. It would be unwise for parents to permit or ignore underage drinking, even in the family home, as it is important for young people to understand the wisdom in abiding the law.

Trust *is a vital element in all relationships.*

When we say that we trust someone, we believe that the relationship is built on mutual respect and faith that the other person will not hurt or deceive us in any way. When we trust, we have confidence and comfort in placing ourselves in the care of another who we believe to be reliable, truthful, and helpful. With trust, there is no room for lies, deception, or illegitimacy. To trust someone is to accept the person forthrightly, with a sense of comfort and support. Trust is a very good thing, and humans need to trust others. It is a sign of good mental health and faith in the goodness of others. Trust is a part of a humble heart, and should not be damaged by untrustworthy people. Therefore, you need to be very careful to make certain that the person you feel is worthy of your trust has integrity, is principled, and is above suspicion. Trust is not merely a thought or a belief. It has something to do with your heart; a confidence and comfort in your humble heart that cannot be described clearly or precisely in words. Your humble heart may silently cry for a long time once you have lost trust in someone. This sorrow reveals that trust is related to your humble heart rather than words, thoughts, and beliefs.

Do not place trust in anyone until you truly know the person very well. If you trust too quickly or for invalid reasons, you may be misled, exploited, or become a victim of the person. A person may look good, respectable, and worthy of your trust and devotion, but looking good does not mean he or she is good. Always be cautious and allow your mind to think carefully and not be swayed by emotions. Keep your feelings in check and thoroughly examine his or her behaviors, beliefs, decision-making powers, honesty, self-respect, and moral principles. If you find the person to be responsible with many good qualities, only then should you place trust in that person with a sense of comfort and confidence. Be aware that trust works two ways, our trust in others and their trust in us. To be a trustful person is an ethical responsibility. By not being trustworthy and faithful, you can lose credibility and respect from your friends, spouse, children, and community. While it is very important not to be misled by untrustworthy people, always make sure that you are completely trustworthy as well.

Never be lured or motivated by your attraction to a person, especially regarding a possible partner. Our desires can fool us by our selfish wants. We may convince ourselves by looking for positive things and disregarding negative ones. Or, we may rationalize the undesirable characteristics as not being important. Asking a mother for details about her son may be fine, but if she says he is a good son, would that be the decision-maker? How could a mother know what her grownup son has been up to? If we were honest with ourselves, we would be wary and dig deeper into finding out more about the possible suitor. If someone very close to you — your parent, sibling, teacher, or trusted friend tries to tell you things about the person you are very interested in, never let your ego or lust prevent you from listening to their advice and concern.

Parents should teach their children about the meaning of trust and how to learn to trust someone in order to avoid being wounded. It can be difficult for adults to see the true inner core of a person, and even more so for a child. Therefore, parents should pay close attention to their children's playmates to make certain they are good, trustworthy friends.

Mindfulness is a useful tool to help think and see more clearly.

By being attentive to how your mind is thinking, reacting, and feeling, you become more alert and aware of the situations you are facing, including personal relationships with others. It is important to learn how to practice mindfulness and self-awareness in order to protect yourself from all sorts of temptations and negative forces around you in everyday life. Mindfulness and self-awareness are extremely useful for correcting yourself and making positive progress in your actions, behaviors, and relationships.

Mindfulness in this context refers to gaining awareness of your own patterns of behavior, including thoughts, emotions, feelings, inclinations, and biased beliefs. Learning to let go of these habits, which are pointless and serve no purpose, will aid you in not being influenced or affected by them. Mindfulness and self-vigilance are undoubtedly an aid in staying away from negative habits, as well as for solving day-to-day problems. At an age when children can begin to comprehend this concept, parents should introduce their off-spring of the importance of mindfulness and self-vigilance.

Self-awareness is closely related to mindfulness.

It means paying close attention to your behavior and your habitual thought patterns. In this context, self-awareness does not mean trying to find out "who you are". Rather, it means being aware of your actions, reactions, moods, impulses, and distractions. It is being able to recognize your ingrained beliefs as simply beliefs, instead of a fundamental core of your being. Virtually all behaviors are spontaneous and inadvertent. By learning how to spot these actions is to become more self-aware. Then, by not allowing bad behaviors and habitual thought patterns to rule your life, you can begin to control your thoughts and actions. To do this, you need to develop the ability to scan or monitor your thinking. Once you recognize that some of your behaviors are negative, you can start to gain greater control over these undesirable behaviors and habits. This will enable you to live more peacefully, with a sense of comfort and self-confidence, not being driven and controlled by your ego.

Often, people may comment about their bad habits by saying: *This is just how I am, and I cannot or will not change. I've been like this for my whole life.* But with reflection, this cannot be possible, as habitual behavior is learned. By being able to understand that it is okay to make mistakes in judgment, and to know how much our thoughts and emotions can affect our behavior, one can then cultivate self-awareness.

Self-respect is another important aspect in our lives.

Self-respect is having a sense of personal integrity; a self-image of oneself that upholds certain positive values. Because of a lack of self-respect, many people end up having difficulties owing to their own behavior, habits, and negative forces in their immediate surroundings. A deep sense of self-respect can act as a restraint, as you think: *This is unbecoming of me.* A strong sense of self-respect can banish your bad habits or temptations for doing wrong or indulging in destructive behaviors such as using drugs, excessive drinking of alcohol, gambling, and anger towards others. To have self-respect takes reflecting on your personal behavior at all times. Self-respect is not about being proud of oneself, but having dignity and integrity in thoughts and actions. The good reasons you have for respecting others should likewise be the same reasons to respect yourself. Never hold others to a higher standard than yourself, nor judge others more harshly than yourself. Self-respect involves knowing the correct way to think and act and following through on those thoughts and actions.

Careful consideration of others is another meaningful objective that should be integrated into your daily life.

Consideration of others is a necessary component for developing respect for others' right to be happy and your moral duty to do no harm to others for any purpose or reason. Consideration of others pertains to having a healthy regard for others' opinions and actions, how your actions may affect others, and others' conceivable approval or disapproval. Together, these two factors — self-respect and careful consideration of others should give you a sense of caution about doing wrong. This will, in turn, deepen your moral discipline and heighten your state of awareness and self-vigilance. Lack of self-respect and lack of consideration of others certainly leaves considerable room in your life for getting into trouble, having problems, and doing harm or wrong to others.

Considering all others as either equal or more important than oneself refers to equanimity and compassion.

Equanimity is a balanced attitude towards all others as being equal to oneself in terms of desiring happiness and not undergoing pain or suffering for even a moment. In this state, there is no moral room to be biased or feel discrimination of either closeness or distance toward a particular person or group. Feelings of prejudice, favoritism, one-sidedness, or intolerance develop from being unreasonably biased, with a blind attachment or aversion to one person or group.

These sentiments often lead to personal problems as well as troubles in our world.

Compassion is an unbiased *feeling* or *wish* for others to be free from all suffering. This involves a willingness to help and serve others with the best effort possible that is within your own capabilities. Compassion is the loftiest and most virtuous ethical principle and is a true avenue for your actions to be highly beneficial to others. It means that you are committed to others' well-being rather than self-serving dedication to oneself. Compassion produces the power to respect others' rights to be happy. It brings a means for you to secure an ethical and peaceful life, free of blame, shame, guilt, and harsh criticism. Compassion is a source of your own happiness as well as a basis for noble actions and deeds. One needs to understand the importance of compassion, as it is one of the highest outcomes of human intelligence. A world lacking in compassion is the sole cause of many man-made problems that are virtually unable to solve or find a remedy for. Compassion has dual positive effects. It motivates you to always be willing to serve others as much as you can. Likewise, it restrains you from doing harm and wrong to others. The outcome is that you are able to be adept at serving others, as well as restraining yourself from doing harm to others, regardless of who they are or whether they are related to you.

~ ~ ~ ~ ~

The ethics emphasized in this book are about living well, doing good deeds, serving others, respecting others' rights to be happy, self-discipline, self-correction, being responsible, honest, loyal, having humility, moderation, harmony, supporting equal treatment for all, pro-justice, pro-peace, and non-violence. It also means being hard working and diligent, honoring elders, parents, and teachers, and leading your life in an utterly harmless manner. An ethical life is all about living, doing, saying, and thinking wholeheartedly in a gentle and wholesome way in relation to everyone.

Ethics determines the final and absolute goodness of a person. It is much more than simply knowing what is "right or wrong" and what is "good or bad". Ethical behavior is more about doing what is right and staying away from that which is bad. This needs careful consideration by analyzing consciously and deliberately individual circumstances and their potential outcome.

There is no such thing as having the "right" to kill or murder another human being. You may have the legal "right" to do so under certain conditions, but this type of right is never an ethical right. Killing another human, even if it is within the law, will have natural consequences in your life. You can never feel good about yourself once you have killed, even in the name of self-defense or in war. Killing does not fit into a wholesome act or an ethical act. A wholesome life, encompassing harmless actions, healthy behaviors, constructive habits, and rational views are the fundamental aspects of social and secular ethics. These qualities are required for your own self-interest and for the well-being of all others, particularly those who are a part of the society in which you live and raise your children.

Some may believe that being ethical will take away a person's rights or freedoms. But nothing could be further from the truth. Believing this is akin to saying that ethics will take away the rights to be a good and harmless person. Often young people, who want a taste of independence from their parents, become confused with *their rights to do* versus *what is right to do*. Being at a legal age to smoke cigarettes or drink alcohol may have them believe that it is their *right and personal choice* to smoke or to drink alcohol as often as they wish. While it may be legal to smoke or drink, the decision of what to do entails more than legality. If that same person develops serious health problems due to smoking or drinking heavily, is it then a *right* to use these substances? It is important to think of the potential consequences, such as being worrisome to the family, a burden for health care providers and insurance, and the possibility of losing one's job.

When we think about our ethical choices, no matter what they may be, it is foremost to consider that *all people are equal* and *as important or even more important* than ourselves. This acknowledgement plays a big part in grounding ourselves in benevolence, unselfishness, and decency for all.

CHAPTER 7

Children's Formal Education

W E ARE LIVING at the beginning of the 21ˢᵗ century; science and technology have reached a stage of extraordinary discoveries and achievements. Yet the basic human problems, hindrances, and hardships remain fundamentally the same, if have not gotten worse. Securing a good education, leading an ethical life, and maintaining mental and emotional stability and health are the fundamental keys for our happiness, success, and for humankind to be categorically distinct from all other living creatures. How then do we go about ensuring that our children can prosper and flourish in these ways?

What is Education?

In this modern and high-tech world, it can be quite difficult to find the human skills needed to implement strategies for success if we do not have a sound and all-embracing education. Likewise, if we do not lead an ethical life, we will not be able to use our education properly. Without sustaining good mental and emotional health, under no circumstance can we have a reliable means to be happy and successful. We cannot be unique and distinct from other living creatures if we do not have the moral discernment and intellectual astuteness needed to make and keep our planet a safe and healthy natural environment for all living beings.

Most parents, and society in general, espouse the need for all children to have a good education. But what does a good education truly entail? Correspondingly, what is the true purpose of formal schooling? These and other questions are not easy to answer, but we need to recognize that there is no one system of education that is absolutely the best to follow. Nevertheless, it should be apparent that education is much more than simply learning to read and write, having a basic understanding of scientific principles and mathematics, or conversing in another language at a basic level. A meaningful education does not mean having all "A's" on a report card, high SAT scores, or being admitted to a prestigious university. An important aspect of being well-educated is being able to broaden our minds and expand our capacity to work for the well-being of everyone to build a prosperous, wholesome, and peaceful world, while reducing the pain and suffering caused by humankind itself. Education should help teach us to be thoughtful, fair-minded, and logical thinkers. Moreover, education should teach us to "connect" our brain, heart, and mind together as "partners" to ensure that our actions take into account both concrete, philosophical, and heartfelt results. One may ask oneself: *What purpose is our individual life if not to better the lives of other living beings?* Certainly no one can solve the world's problems, but by taking actions individually, every one of us can do things that will help the world become a better place to live, thrive and find comfort.

While it is admirable to study diligently and succeed in securing a successful occupation, this should not be the only outcome we seek. By thinking from early on about how our thoughts and actions can potentially affect positive changes in the world, we can lessen the grip of our own desires and aspirations. This can potentially lead us to care more for others — even strangers or adversaries — to help improve the quality of life for all.

His Holiness the Dalai Lama frequently has said:

Material-based modern education is not enough for the individual to be happy and successful, or for the world to be peaceful and in harmony. Modern education is not a complete form of education, and therefore needs to be changed and improved with a sense of urgency.

At first glance, we may believe that *material-based modern education* is schooling for the elite: an Ivy League education, or medical or law school. We could surmise that our educational problems lie primarily with the establishment and the privileged classes. This certainly may contribute to societal issues, but do other types of education, such as community college and trade school education necessarily foster care and concern for others to help make the world more peaceful and harmonious? Ultimately, virtually all forms of modern secular education are material based.

Why Do We Need Formal Education?

What then is lacking in modern formal education that could help people become both successful and valuable contributors to society? In essence, the ideas and concepts that we are taught should actually help our minds and hearts develop moral refinement and provide us with tools of wisdom to construct a more peaceful and livable world, rather than merely focusing on job skills and other knowledge.

Moral refinement and wisdom are no light topics for anyone, let alone children of school age. These matters can take many years of sincere and serious contemplation to master. Despite this, and perhaps because of it, these concepts should begin to be discussed at an early age. Moral lessons can be introduced in kindergarten or first grade, and progress through high school, with more serious study at the college level. Young children can certainly learn right from wrong in such matters as stealing and lying, or the thoughtfulness of not putting oneself first in all circumstances. Later, the wisdom of why such things are important, and not only right from wrong, can be discussed from a more philosophical level. By teaching secular morality and wisdom to school aged children throughout their schooling, such values can become more customary and commonplace in children and society in general.

A well-grounded formal education, with job training skills for every person, is certainly necessary to survive and succeed in this world. However, regardless of what we are studying, be it law, nursing, carpentry, computer science, or brick laying, formal education should include ethics, morals, and proper conduct to ensure that we can all take part in making this world a safe, kind, and wholesome place to live.

How Should Our Children be Educated?

In Chapter Six we provided relevant information and advice on how to lead a more ethical and upstanding life. Here we will concentrate on the academic side of life, with various strategies and thought-provoking questions on how our children should be educated in school. Worldwide, systems of primary and secondary education offer very different options concerning many aspects of instruction, including the age a child must begin schooling, curriculum, compulsory number of years of attendance, grading policies and standards, different streams for students based on ability and other factors, regulations regarding home schooling, discipline guidelines, length of the school day and school year, and access to tertiary education. Notwithstanding that there is no easy "solution" or consensus as to what should or should not be changed in the American system of education, it might be helpful to examine two countries that are considered as having very good outcomes in educating their children. While no system is failsafe or perfect, there may be some features to consider that may improve the learning outcomes for more children in our society.

The two countries we will look at are Finland and Japan, which offer very different styles of schooling. We will assess these systems in general terms, as within each system are significant variations. A true assessment would need learned members of society to develop a possible plan.

Finland:

Finland is considered to have one of the best and most innovative educational systems in the world. The education system is decentralized, with teachers and principals primarily responsible for how subjects are taught, budget acquisitions, and recruitment of staff. There are different pay scales for teachers, depending on the level taught, with basic education schools having the lowest pay, vocational/technical schools next, and upper secondary schools the highest. Universities also have a fair amount of autonomy, with their own administration, student admission requirements, and content of degree programs. Most education is publicly funded, except for non-EU students.

In elementary through high school, the focus is more on learning than testing. Teachers are largely responsible for the assessment of their students, using techniques such as frequent meetings with each student to see if they comprehend the subject matter. Very few written tests are given to students during their school years. To apply for admission to tertiary institutions (both university and technical schools), students are required to take an entrance examination, with admission to these intuitions based on merit.

One unique regulation in Finland is that children are not permitted to begin school until age seven. They believe that before age seven children are not ready for school. Instead, they believe that play is most important. Many parents send their children to daycare during these early years, which is typically subsidized by the government. Children attend basic education for nine years — from age seven to age sixteen. Upper secondary school is voluntary and is for an additional three years. This schooling prepares students for the matriculation exam to enter a tertiary school. Upper secondary school is divided into academic and vocational/technical streams. The school year is 190 days, with classes meeting on Monday through Friday. Students take a national core curriculum, including Finnish or Swedish (both are considered as national languages), a foreign language, the second national language (Finnish or Swedish), mathematics, science, history/civics, and arts, crafts, and sports.

Outcomes:

On the 2015 PISA assessment, Finland ranked 5th in science, 13th in math, and 4th in reading (out of 70 countries).[1]

Per "Country Notes" from the Organization for Economic Cooperation and Development (OECD):[2]

- Vocational education is more common in Finland than other OECD countries
- Enrollment in pre-primary education is below OECD averages
- Average teachers' salaries are below the OECD average

Japan:

In Japan, the division of schooling is based on the U.S. model, with 6 years of elementary school, 3 years of middle school, and 3 years of high school. There are special schools for the blind, deaf, and children with certain handicaps or disabilities. Attendance is compulsory for grades 1 — 9. High school attendance is not compulsory, but students must graduate from high school to apply to any higher education institute. Public education is free for grades 1 — 9. High school education is not free; even public high schools charge tuition. Japanese law prohibits home schooling.

The Ministry of Education determines the curriculum for elementary school through high school. However, individual schools do have some input regarding the curriculum per the needs of their students. Students typically study ten or more subjects, including

---

[1] The Organisation for Economic Co-operation and Development. (2015) PISA 2015 key findings for Finland. http://www.oecd.org/pisa/pisa-2015-finland.htm

[2] The Organisation for Economic Co-operation and Development. (2016) Finland – Country Note – Education at a Glance 2016: OECD Indicators. http://gpseducation.oecd.org/content/eagcountrynotes/eag2016_cn_fin.pdf

Japanese, English, mathematics, sciences, social studies, arts, and moral studies. There are very few options for elective courses. Moral education is imbued in the national curriculum, as the Japanese government believes that education includes character formation as well as other ethical principles. Children are also taught manners, self-control, tenacity, and respect for others. Parental involvement and responsibility for their children is of utmost importance and includes diligence in having their children behave well and succeed in their studies.

The school year begins in April and ends in March. Summer break is for 40 days, but teachers and students are required to attend school for certain days during the summer break. The school year ranges from 210 to 240 days per year, with many students taking evening tutoring classes in addition to the regular school day. These additional classes are even for young children in elementary school. Some schools also have classes on Saturday mornings, but typically have every other Saturday off.

Athletics are for afterschool fun and exercise; there are no school teams to compete against other schools. Students eat lunch in their classrooms with their teacher. At the end of the school day, all students clean their classrooms, the toilets, and hallways. They also tend the outside grounds to keep them clean and grow flowers and other plants.

One examination at the completion of high school determines if a student will be admitted to the college or university of their choice. Therefore, there is a high degree of seriousness instilled in studying and achieving to a high level from elementary school through high school.

Outcomes:

On the 2015 PISA assessment, Japan ranked 2nd in science, 5th in math, and 8th in reading (out of 70 countries).[3]

---

[3] The Organisation for Economic Co-operation and Development. (2015) PISA 2015 key findings for Japan. http://www.oecd.org/pisa/pisa-2015-japan.htm

Per "Country Notes" from the Organization for Economic Co-operation and Development (OECD):[4]

- Pre-primary attendance much higher than other OECD countries, although not free
- Teachers' salaries far exceed OECD averages
- Class sizes are among the largest of OECD countries

United States:

Every state in the U.S. has a separate system of education, but along with differences there are many similarities.

The federal government contributes approximately 10% for K-12 education; the remainder is funded by the states and localities. Each state has its own department of education that determines school regulations, salaries, curriculum, attendance policies, and other matters. Below the state level, local municipalities also have governance over schools, with school boards elected by the public or appointed by the local governing bodies. Property taxes play an important role in the funding of schools.

In general, compulsory education is for ages five or six to age sixteen, with some states requiring attendance to age seventeen or eighteen. U.S. government regulations state that all children are guaranteed the right to free public education for elementary and secondary school until age eighteen, including undocumented children. All states use a 12-year system of education, divided into elementary, middle school, and high school. In addition, many states offer special programs or schools for special needs children, including learning difficulties, emotional and behavioral problems, and children with physical needs. Most public schools offer programs or classes for gifted children.

---

[4] The Organisation for Economic Co-operation and Development. (2016) Japan – Country Note – Education at a Glance 2016: OECD Indicators. https://read.oecd-ilibrary.org/education/education-at-a-glance-2016/japan_eag-2016-65-en#page1

Day care and pre-school programs are not free to the general public. However, the Head Start program, founded in the 1960s under the Johnson administration, offers pre-school programs for children from birth to age five for low-income families as defined by the U.S. government poverty guidelines. The programs are free and include early learning, health, family well-being, and home visits.

The U.S. has a high level of parental involvement in their children's schooling, especially for elementary school children. The Parent Teacher Association (PTA) was founded in 1897 as the National Congress of Mothers (NCM). From the onset, the NCM welcomed everyone, regardless of "color, creed, or condition". The organization focused on the quality of education as well as children's health, child labor laws, and the juvenile justice system.

One unique part of the U.S. education system is access to higher education. In general, a majority of community colleges offer open admission. There also are quite a few colleges and universities that also offer admission as long as the applicant has a high school diploma or a General Development Certificate (GED). Although colleges and universities are not officially ranked, there are many levels of selectivity and prestige among these institutions. Admission to colleges may be based on required courses taken in high school, class rank or GPA, and the SAT or ACT examinations.

Outcomes:

On the 2015 PISA assessment, U.S. ranked 25th in science, 40th in math, and 24th in reading (out of 70 countries).[5]

---

[5] The Organisation for Economic Co-operation and Development. (2015) PISA 2015 key findings for the United States. http://www.oecd.org/pisa/pisa-2015-united-states.htm

Per "Country Notes" from the Organization for Economic Co-operation and Development (OECD):[6]

- Pre-primary attendance lower than other OECD countries
- Teachers' salaries higher than OECD averages
- Higher than average annual spending per student than other OECD countries

Consideration of Findings

The above information gives us much to think about. Is our educational system in need of a complete overhaul, or just some adjustments? Who should determine what changes should be made, and how to implement them? Students in Japan and Finland both show a high level of achievement in the subjects that were tested on the PISA exams. Yet both have very different styles and standards of education, as well as very different cultures. Japanese classrooms have a larger number of students than most countries, they learn mainly by listening to the instructor, wear uniforms, and have a rigorous curriculum. Finnish children do not attend school until age seven, they do not take tests, the classroom is less formal, and class sizes are quite small. Would implementing any of these factors make the U.S. educational system better?

Some say that there are many disadvantaged students in Vietnam and Latvia, yet their students do well. Others say that American students fall behind, give up, and drop out.

Why are these things happening? Perhaps there is too much criticism of our educational system, and too much blame placed on concerns such as "bad" teachers, inadequate funding, classroom size, low teacher salaries, or outdated instructional methods. There certainly is room for improvement in all of these matters, but what is

---

[6] The Organisation for Economic Co-operation and Development. (2016) United States – Country Note – Education at a Glance 2016: OECD Indicators. https://read.oecd-ilibrary.org/education/education-at-a-glance-2016/united-states_eag-2016-86-en#page1

taught and how much students are interested in learning are fundamental in receiving a good education. Perhaps the key is to look at our culture, especially regarding what formal education means to Americans.

In the U.S., many parents are undeniably interested in their children's education; wanting their children to get good grades, participate in school activities or clubs, play on school sports teams, have friends, and be accepted to a good college. All of these objectives are good and may help students to have a pleasant experience in school. But, do parents take serious consideration of what a good education should include? Is education primarily meant to get good grades, participate in clubs or sports, or even to be admitted to a good college? Or, is education meant to learn, gain insight, develop a quest for more understanding of the subject, and seek answers to complex ideas. How many parents, students, or even teachers think about what being educated means? Do they consider the type of knowledge a student should gain in learning Spanish, biology, or mathematics, or how the student later in life could possibly use that knowledge?

As shown in the PISA results, U.S. high school students do not excel in mathematics compared to many other countries — coming in 40th out of 70 countries. Why are U.S. students so far behind other countries in this subject? It may be the level of difficulty and comprehensiveness of the coursework. What is actually taught in algebra I compared to the same course in other countries? The same is true for other courses, such as foreign language and sciences. In addition, in other countries many subjects are often studied for a longer period of time, typically for three to six years. In the U.S. students typically take one year each of biology, chemistry, and physics. In many other countries they may take all three sciences each year for three to six years. The same holds true for foreign languages.

To improve our education system, we may need to look at ourselves and our society. "Failing schools" cannot entirely be blamed on an outmoded education system, large class size, or sub-standard teachers and facilities. If our culture does not value or emphasize acquiring knowledge, wisdom, academic attainment, and self-discipline, it may be very difficult to produce an educated society. Too much interest in sports and activities in school, and spending free time watching TV, movies, or playing video games does nothing to promote these values. Without these ideals strongly appreciated in society, what are young people going to aspire to become?

Here are some serious questions we need to consider regarding our children and their education:

- Centralize education with the same basic curriculum.
- Distribute educational funding evenly, not based on real estate taxes.
- Create a better atmosphere for learning with a focus on proper behavior and respect for the teachers and each other.
- Have subjects be more rigorous, with added tutoring from teachers.
- Do away with "grade inflation."
- Require all schools to have physical education, art education, and music education.
- Eliminate school team sports and replace them with intramural sports.
- Limit summer vacation to 6 weeks for students.
- Discourage after-school jobs; emphasize that school is a full-time job for students.
- Do not permit students to drive themselves to school.
- Remove cell phones from the students' possession while classes are in session.

We need to be attentive in how we understand the importance of education and its functions for individuals and society. Along with being a place to get good grades and earn a diploma, our schools need to nurture and cultivate in our students the desire to learn how to think, make good decisions, get along with others, be diligent, open-minded, and respectful of parents, teachers, and all others. Each one of us is ultimately responsible for what we allow our mind to take in, absorb, and reflect on. We alone must think about what we are presented by our teachers, our parents, and in our books. No one can make us study the book that is placed in front of us, listen to the lecture our teachers give, or the advice of our parents. We can turn on the learning switch or turn it off at whim. Every person has the power to see the brilliant light of discovery and insight or be blinded by the darkness of ignorance. It's ultimately up to every one of us. Since the founding of the National Congress of Mothers in the late 1800s, the U.S. has truly been concerned with the education and welfare of the country's children. It is essential for us to review the visions that these women had and make sure never to fail them or our children in fulfilling their dreams.

CHAPTER 8

Home Discipline

T HE MODERN WORLD is a very noisy place, with vehicles racing down the roads, TVs seemingly always turned on, radios blaring deafening music, and cell phones ringing away even in schools, restaurants, and places of worship. We are constantly surrounded by noise; finding it more and more difficult to locate a quiet place to rest and relax. All of this noise can be both annoying and over-stimulating. These reactions can have repercussions in our daily life, leading us to become distracted, irritated, and frustrated. We may also find that we are unable to focus, prioritize, and make good decisions.

For children, a noisy environment will most likely be a hindrance to listening, studying, and learning, as well as relaxing and sleeping soundly. It is very unlikely for us to live in a quiet and peaceful world unless we move to an isolated place, with few distractions. Since this is not feasible for most of us, it is essential that we make our home environment a haven for our children to enable them to learn and eventually succeed in this world. In the home setting, we need to teach our children good habits and responsible behavior — *self-discipline* — that can help them learn strategies to cope and flourish outside the home and in the school environment.

Parents should not wait until their children are of school age to begin to teach good habits and self-control. When children are very young, one of the first things we should begin to teach them is how to remain quiet and calm, at first for very short periods of time. Every day, for just a few minutes, we should guide our children to practice silence, stillness, and calmness. Begin by making the home a quiet place, by turning off the TV and radio, putting away cell phones, and closing the windows, if necessary. Then, simply sit still with your child beside you. After a few days or weeks, this will become a pleasant habit; something for you and your child to look forward to. By making this practice a daily routine, it will become a normal part of the day. Once your child is of school age, this routine can be an excellent way to settle down after dinner before beginning homework.

One factor in a child's success in school is a parent's consistent participation and engagement in their child's schooling, including monitoring homework. The end of the school day does not mean that learning is over for the day. A parent's guidance with homework assignments, by directing the child's mind and effort to learn, is very important. Parents should frequently check on how well their child is doing in school to find out what may be lacking if their child is not doing well. Children who know that their parents are communicating with their teachers most likely will strive to do better. Monitoring what children do in school, along with a healthy home environment, will contribute to children being good students who are motivated and interested in learning.

Many children and their parents put a strong emphasis on activities, both in and out of school. While activities are useful in many ways, they should never be put above education. Activities are often useful in helping children from getting into trouble through lack of anything to do. Sports activities may help children maintain a healthy lifestyle and learn important skills such as swimming, running, or tennis. Volunteering is an excellent way for children to learn about caring for others in need, such as the elderly, sick or disabled people, or abandoned animals. Being involved in activities can also help children form good friendships. However, placing too much emphasis on activities may cause unintentional disregard for studying and doing homework. Proper home discipline, improving learning skills, and motivation should be the prime considerations, with daily activities allowed when there is time above and beyond schooling, studying, and homework.

One important note regarding activities for students — colleges, especially more selective ones, strongly recommend high school students to demonstrate participation in numerous activities, both in and out of the school environment. Activities may include sports, clubs, internships, shadowing professionals, and volunteering at places for the needy. Without these types of activities, even students who excel in high school may be rejected by certain colleges. Many admissions offices are looking for well-rounded students, and that includes much more than good grades. Therefore, these factors need to be taken into consideration.

Note: Overseeing and aiding your children with homework does not mean doing their homework for them, as children must ultimately be responsible for completing their homework assignments on their own.

Proper home discipline is especially important when it comes to having children succeed in school. It is important to understand that home discipline does not mean chores typically done by certain members of the family. For example, mother cooks the meals and father does the dishes or father does the grocery shopping and mother pays the monthly bills. These types of tasks are not home discipline, but rather day-to-day mundane responsibilities that must be done to manage a household. Likewise, home discipline is not punishment or chastisement for not following rules or acting badly. Home discipline involves a *structure* of self-motivation, self-restraint, and orderliness by each family member. It is being responsible for one's physical and mental actions and is meant to bring a certain order and stability to the household. It is like a well-oiled machine that runs smoothly without stalling or breaking down.

This type of structure is a key element in developing a well-organized system in the home for everyone to be able to thrive.

With a positive structure, children can develop the ability to concentrate on what is necessary to be successful and happy. Children will be better equipped to study and learn schoolwork, as well as cultivating respectful behaviors at home and in the outside world. By establishing a framework of structure in the home, children can learn to form good habits and integrate them into their normal daily routine.

This is possible because a child's mind is "programmed" into configurations that create a sense of self-awareness, self-correction, and self-mastery. This function of the mind allows a child to understand and realize what needs to be done, what can be done, and what should be done now without putting off until tomorrow what ought to have been done today. This "programming" is influenced by what a child sees, hears, and experiences. Contrarily, if a child is living in a disorderly and chaotic home, with an inability to cultivate attentiveness or concentration, he or she will most likely do things randomly and absorb information in a haphazard way. The child will not be able to comprehend why he or she is having so much difficulty learning, leading to frustration and a defeated attitude towards learning. This is why it is so important to have children exposed to orderly home discipline.

One aspect of structure that may be rather evident is to have all members of the family help to keep the home neat, clean, and organized. As well as being a healthier environment, it simply helps to make things easier to find and leads to less confusion and distraction. Being part of the family, children need to understand the importance of contributing to the upkeep of the home. At a relatively young age children can learn to tidy up their rooms, help with easy cooking, and do some yard work, such as helping to plant flowers and vegetables. As they mature, they can give more assistance to their parents. Children who are more engaged with family activities and interactions with their parents at home fare far better than those who stay away from home most of their free time hanging out with friends.

With a structured home environment as the base, home discipline encompasses mutual respect for each family member by listening carefully and with an open mind to one another and making certain that each family member understands the emotional sensitivities of the other family members. This type of atmosphere in the home creates a sense of unity and conscientiousness, with awareness, deep concern, and humility for each other's interests and needs.

In many homes, the TV set is always on. If the TV is not on, it may feel as though something is missing. This should not be the case. Parents need to discuss with each other what television shows should be watched by both parents and children. Guidelines need to be established for when the TV can be turned on. Why, for example, should families be watching TV while eating a meal? That is when family members should talk about their day, share information, and enjoy being together. Television is not necessarily bad, but parents need to scrutinize what shows are appropriate and worth watching. TV should not be used as a babysitter or to keep children away from parents who are occupied with other things. No one in the family should watch TV while children are doing their homework or studying, as this is extremely detrimental to a child's concentration. In addition to watching less TV, family members should agree to spend less time alone on smart phones, computers, or playing video games. If scrutinized honestly, these devices can be very addictive and waste a great deal of valuable time in mindless activities. Substitute these devices with word games, board games, or outdoor activities such as going for walks or playing badminton.

Another way to support your child is to set up a small library in a quiet place in the home, with a comfortable chair and study table. It is also helpful to buy or build a bookcase for easy access to books and other materials needed for homework. Make sure to include supplies, such as a small calculator, ruler, pencils, sharpener, and eraser. If affordable, a small computer and art supplies can also be beneficial. With a place specially furnished for your child, he or she will be gratified to have the necessary materials needed to study, do homework, read, and relax. They will certainly have a good feeling to be at home with loving and caring parents.

Maintaining a quiet and peaceful home can give rise to an atmosphere conducive for having children think, reflect, and analyze what is going on in different aspects of their lives. Children will have a steadier mood, be more willing to help out at home, study their lessons, and learn about the world around them. Creating a positive, pleasant atmosphere is the best way to encourage children to be responsible. Forcing or ordering children to do homework or help with household chores is not positive and can result in agitating a child's mind. This can stifle a child's natural interest in learning.

Some practical matters concerning the home environment for children include:

- Night owls need to be considerate and be quiet when children are sleeping.
- If serious discussions are necessary, wait until the children have completed their homework and are asleep before bringing up such topics.
- Similarly, do not yell, shout, or even laugh loudly during homework time, as these reactions can create agitation or disturbances in a child's mind, thus making them unable to learn with a calm and settled mind.

Along with taking care of the home environment to support your child's study habits, plan on taking weekly trips to the local library. Libraries are wonderful places for young children and parents to share quality time together and to help encourage your child to foster good reading habits. Allow your child to "window shop" and choose books he or she is interested in reading. Also help your child to select some books that are more academic, such as history, science, ethics, or biographies written for children. This way, a trip to the library can be both fun and educational. Make sure to take time to read the books along with your younger children. For older children, parents may choose to read a few of the books their teens are reading and then discuss with them the themes and lessons to be learned from the books.

On the surface, it may appear that setting times for children to go to bed and get up in the morning, to have meals, do homework, and take a shower are overly structured. It may seem that this is too authoritarian and could make children feel stressed. However, the opposite can be true, especially if children are taught how important it is to be well-rested and ready for the next day. For example — if your child gets a good night's sleep, he or she will go to school with more motivation to learn. If homework is scheduled for a certain time, it will become a normal routine or habit. Taking a shower at the end of the day and then spending good quality time with parents and other family members can be relaxing. This is the time to share stories, perhaps play a game, or go for a walk. Then, at bedtime, the child will be ready for the following day. When all of these practices are present in the home environment, and all family members are pleasant and respectful to each other, positive growth will occur. This is what is meant by *home discipline*. By disregarding these important points, it may be much more difficult for your children to succeed in their educational undertakings. Even if a child is accepted into college, the habits of not studying and learning will follow the child to this level of education. Eventually the lack of diligence and self-discipline will become evident, and it may be more difficult to remedy this learned behavior at this time.

*An important note: We need to be reminded that **all children** can be taught how to learn. We simply need to **decipher the code**.*

CHAPTER 9

How to Handle
Family Problems

I N PREVIOUS PORTIONS of the book, we have discussed many issues regarding family life, including the role and interaction of spouses and their children, discipline, education, healthy lifestyles, and other matters. In this chapter, we will reflect on several common issues and problems related to family life and try to provide suggestions for various problems that may arise in all families. Many of these problems emerge from the root of the relationship between family members. Therefore, each family member should take full responsibility for their thoughts and actions in order to avoid creating conditions for problems to crop up. Generally, there can be many types of causes and conditions for problems to arise in family life.

Family life can be worthy and very rewarding, but it can also be a place where many problems may occur. When you marry, your life becomes a complex, interconnected framework with your spouse. This loss of individuality opens the door for a variety of problems from the day you tie the knot. From the very beginning, you have lost 50% of your freedom and singularity in order to construct a married life. Once children arrive, your responsibilities take on a far more serious nature, as you need to care for innocent and needy babies and children. The family unit begins the day two people form a bond in marriage, based on love and a commitment to support one another and stand together in times of happiness and tragedy. The newlyweds may have a child within a year or two and eventually the couple may have several offspring. The love bond between the husband and wife and the blood relationship formed with their offspring creates a family. Bound together by living and growing in the same home, they share a sense of belonging without the rigidness of 'mine' that prevents another family member from using something when the need arises.

No one is immune to family-related problems. They are prevalent in the richest and the poorest families, and from the most developed to the least developed countries. I have witnessed broken families all over the world during my global travels in the past 30 years. I've also encountered many happy families with deep bonds of love, care, support, respect, and understanding of each family member's emotional needs and personalities.

A happy family unquestionably makes a home feel like an idyllic place, filled with the richness of love, care, support, respect, harmony, success, calmness, and soothing energy in the hearts and minds of each family member. This ambience fosters an environment where the family members find a certain joy of living together, irrespective of external circumstances. When problems do arise, which they certainly will, happy families typically find an inner strength to help find solutions to the situation. They also tend to work together during difficult times, rather than isolate themselves from the other family members. It is important for more troubled or unhappy families to recognize these good traits and learn how to handle problems within the family so that the unit does not fall apart and break into separate, lonely people.

A wholesome and healthy family is vital, as this tiny unit of humankind can have far-reaching effects. Healthy families make for healthy communities, which in turn make for a healthier world. Conversely, dysfunctional families are not only an unhealthy unit, but can add to problems for individuals, the community and the wider world. Therefore, a family — a group of blood-related members of a household — is a fundamental unit of society and has a social/ethical responsibility to care for and support one another for the well-being of the group as well as the wider community.

Our present-day society has undergone many changes that have influenced the structure, values, attitudes, and behaviors of the household unit. This has led to stresses that were not often seen in former generations. This seemingly abrupt transformation of the nuclear family has led to more and more disruptive behavior of some family members, especially among parents and their offspring. These situations can lead to less cohesion or eventually a breakdown in the family unit.

We will discuss some of the most common reasons in this chapter. It is worth noting that in order to build a relatively happy family, each family member must understand the following unfavorable conditions and then make a serious effort to avoid them.

Common problems spouses face:

- Unfaithfulness
- Dishonesty
- Failure to give needed attention and respect to the other spouse
- Financial discord
- Lack of mutual agreement in decision-making
- Belief that divorce or separation is normal and acceptable

These problems appear to be quite different, but they all have "common threads" that relate to each other. In order to understand this, the husband and wife need to discuss and decide what *fundamental principles* they, as a married couple, must have to maintain a happy and wholesome marriage. Is it necessary for the wife and husband to agree on everything? That would certainly be very difficult and even restrictive. For example, would they have to like the exact same food, style of clothing, or type of music to live happily ever after? Better and more wisely, shouldn't each partner agree to have certain *principles* for each of them to uphold? Wouldn't this be more valuable than the popular "pre-nuptial agreement" used by one spouse to hold on to his or her precious possessions in case the marriage falls apart? So, what may the "common threads" be in the problems listed above? Perhaps they may include a lack of *integrity, justness, trustworthiness,* and *dependability.*

Let's look at a few of the situations individually, beginning with "unfaithfulness". If one spouse was being lured into having an affair, could it be stopped if he or she reflected on their agreed marriage principles to uphold? Would having an affair have integrity, or be just? Would the unfaithful spouse be worthy of trust or dependability? Certainly not. As for lack of agreement in making decisions, we first need to understand that the couple needn't agree on *everything,* as stated above. However, things that the couple should agree on are matters that affect both partners. Take the example of buying a car. One spouse wants an expensive luxury model, while the other spouse is concerned about the cost, insurance, and is an unnecessary purchase. This is a case where the couple needs to come to an agreement, as the decision will affect both partners. You may ask how is integrity a reason to buy or not to buy a luxury car? Integrity involves doing the right thing, above and beyond your personal wants or desires. Is it just (or fair) to spend a large amount of money on a car when the family may have other more pressing needs? Being trustworthy means to be principled and upright, and dependable means to be sensible and responsible. Both partners should reflect on all of these qualities in order to make good decisions in their married life.

The same reasoning can be used with the other problems listed above, and various issues that may arise in a marriage. If these qualities are kept in the mind of each spouse, potential problems may be avoided or solved without too much stress in the marriage relationship. The fundamental principles described here are only suggestions; they can be modified to meet each couple's standards and beliefs.

Common problems parents face regarding their young children:

- Disagreements about proper discipline
- Neglecting parental responsibilities
- Favoring one child over the others

With young children, the responsibility primarily lies with the parents regarding behavioral issues, as children need to be nurtured and guided in the right direction by their attentive and loving parents. It is of utmost importance for parents to agree on the way to raise their offspring. Disagreement between parents in these matters can be very harmful and confusing for children. That being said, if one parent is not acting appropriately, the other parent must take action to remedy the situation. If the spouses are not in agreement, it may be necessary to consult with a family member, clergy, or professional counselor for advice and help.

Common problems children have with their parents:

- Being disrespectful to one or both parents
- Unwilling to assist with household chores
- Not listening to a parent's advice and wisdom

Once children reach a certain age, about age 7 or 8, they should begin to understand *empathy* — the sensitivity towards others' needs and feelings that ought to be responded to and cared about. While some children seem to have a more natural empathic nature, all children should be taught to be aware of this human characteristic and knowingly develop it. By teaching young children about empathy, both by explanations, examples, and in books, many of the issues children may have of being disrespectful, unwilling to help with chores, and not listening to their parents may be avoided. Understanding and being exposed to the concept of empathy can help a child realize that mom is tired and needs help in preparing dinner. Or dad has the flu and would like a cup of soothing tea. When children are more caring, they will be much more willing to cooperate and help mom, dad, and others. There are quite a few books written for children to learn about empathy, which you can find by searching online or in your local library. The earlier you begin to explain the concept of empathy to your children, the better.

Problems older children have with their parents:

- Using alcohol, drugs, cigarettes, and other illegal or harmful substances
- Driving while intoxicated, speeding, and other dangerous behaviors
- Moodiness or depression

Once your offspring reach a certain age, often nearing puberty, a streak of independence may emerge. While this is generally quite normal and a sign of growing up, pre-teens and teenagers can face much more serious problems than younger children. These may include risk-taking behaviors, such as experimenting with alcohol, drugs, cigarettes, sex, and dangerous driving. While these may seem to be commonplace, never take the stance that, *Kids will be kids, and this is normal behavior.* Or, *There isn't much I can do to prevent these things.* Parents may believe that once their children are this age, they do not need as much care or attention as when they were younger. The opposite is most likely the case. While older children do need to be trusted and allowed to be at home alone for a few hours during the daytime, they should never be alone for long periods of time or overnight. Parents should plan good, supervised activities with their children and friends, especially for pre-teens and younger teens (under age 16). Parents should also have a "family first" rule by having dinners together, staying home on school nights, participating in family gatherings, holidays, and religious attendance. By being diligent parents, teenagers will be less likely to engage in risk-taking behaviors.

Many children going through puberty may become moody, stubborn, and upset from time to time. With love, caring attention, and communication, parents can help their children through these difficult periods. However, if your child displays more extreme reactions that become frequent behavior, such as anger, aggression, re-fusing to follow rules, or consumed with self-centeredness, you may need to seek professional help. A "troubled teen" comes in many forms, such as doing poorly in school, running away from home, drug or alcohol abuse, or being a "loner". Recognize these "red flags" and take necessary steps to help your child. Although many teens will overcome these problems, some may struggle and cause pain and turmoil for themselves and others into their adult years.

Problems adult children have with their parents:

- Understanding that the parents' home is no longer their home
- Being involved in the parents' finances
- Disrespecting family religious and cultural traditions, and political and social values
- Not supporting parents when in need, especially elderly parents
- Asking or demanding financial or other help

Once children are grown and educated, it may feel as though your parental responsibilities are over. You've done your best to raise upstanding, hardworking, and loving children. You most likely will not see your adult child as often as before, but the family bond remains strong and healthy. This, hopefully, will be the outcome for all of your hard work as a parent. In spite of your diligence, love, and care, there may be cases where adult children are a cause for concern regarding their behavior. This can be a most difficult time to know how to handle these situations: *Do we compel him or her to solve their own problems?* Or, *Do we step in and do what we can to help?* There is no easy answer, and every situation is different. How-ever, being honest and forthright with your adult child about their behavior is probably both prudent and necessary.

As suggested above in "Common Problems Facing Spouses", par-ents and their adult children need to discuss and decide what *fun-damental principles* they should have to maintain a happy and wholesome relationship. What standards should the parents and adult children uphold towards each other? In this case, perhaps *respect, dignity, honesty,* and *setting boundaries* are wise choices. Both parents and their adult children should understand that you are not each other's best friends. Parents are still parents, who should be treated with utmost respect. Adult children are not their parents' equals. What exactly does this mean? It means that the adult child should treat the parents' home, financial affairs, religious convictions, political beliefs, and other matters as private — the adult child has no business getting involved in these concerns with their parents. If the relationship holds to the standards of respect, dignity, honesty, and setting boundaries, these problems should never arise.

> *Note regarding financial matters: If a parent is suffering from dementia or another debilitating illness, the adult child, with assistance from other family members or a lawyer, may need to assist with the parent's financial matters.*

Difficult situations that relate to behavioral problems are more challenging to handle. These may include adult children not caring for their elderly parents, demanding money or other things that parents are not responsible for giving, or acting out in inappropriate ways. With these types of situations, there may be very little that the parents can do to change the behavior of their adult child. Try not to feel guilty or excuse your child's bad actions out of love for your adult child. Accepting unsuitable conduct will not help the situation. It is better to be honest with your adult child and simply state that the way that he or she is acting is not appropriate. It may feel difficult to "let go" of the situation, but as they are now adults that may be the best solution for dealing with the problem.

Some practical suggestions about how to deal with family issues include:

- Decide which problems to dismiss and which ones need to be addressed. Trivial issues are not worth focusing on.

- Be honest, as honest as you can be. Did your spouse really do the things you claim he or she did? Is your child (youngster or adult child) truly out of line? Are you denying that there really is a problem that you are trying to ignore, hoping it will simply go away?
- Let go of your ego — no one has to "win" the argument.
- Counseling may help, but not always. Counselors can never completely know or understand the entire history or dynamics of your family.
- Don't run away or hide from problems, but don't let them control your life.
- If you are chronically upset with your spouse after trying diligently to work out the problems, it may be best to agree to end the relationship.
- Remember — sometimes good parents have bad children, and sometimes bad parents have good children. Hopefully, most of the time good parents have good children. It's up to each and every one of us to have a happy family — parents and children alike.

~ ~ ~ ~ ~

Families are an important part of society. It can be rewarding and desirable to live together, helping and supporting each other like ants and bees. With a united effort, a happy and healthy family will survive and thrive. Each family member should take full responsibility to avoid creating causes and conditions that give rise to problems in the family. The most consequential and prevalent causes that create problems are mentioned clearly above. Every family member should take into consideration the possible ramifications of such actions and remind oneself of them often. As a parent, you need to be like a rock at the bottom of the ocean — steady, balanced, and secure as your parental role necessitates. It may sometimes seem difficult or even impossible to remain unshakeable at all times, as our emotions and desires can move us to act in detrimental and unwholesome ways. But developing the where-withal to circumvent the causes and conditions that can lead to problems emerging due to selfishness, dishonesty, disrespect, un-faithfulness, or irresponsibility is far better than seeking solutions to remedy family problems once they emerge.

There are many sensible sayings about preventing problems. Some common ones are:

- Prevention is better than all cures.
- Carefulness is better than being sorry.
- Building a strong wall before a flood comes to your house is better than dealing with the mess of the flood.
- Generating a positive force before an evil force arises is better than attempting to avert the evil force.
- And finally, as an ancient proverb states: Family members should not react to a problem like eggs rolling around in a pot of boiling water. Instead, allow your mind and your reactions to cool down. Then, the problem will slowly calm down just like the rolling eggs will settle down once the water stops boiling and begins to cool down. Only then can one see the problem more clearly to help find a solution for it.

Occasionally, due to unfortunate circumstances, one may create a cause for a problem to arise that may affect the well-being of the family members. Once a problem surfaces, one should not ignore it, nor try to escape from it, nor bury it with deceptions and lies to other family members. Doing so can make it impossible to find a solution for the problem and can even make it become more complicated and serious over time. There can be a variety of family problems, based on the causes and conditions from which they arise. Each situation may require a different solution, based on the nature of the problem. For this reason, it is not prudent to suggest one remedy as a panacea. Generally speaking, it is best not to handle family problems with anger, frustration, blame, criticism, or in a defensive manner. This way of dealing with the issues may only contribute to

more problems, and the family may never find any agreeable remedy for the existing troubles. Unsolvable family problems can destroy
the well-being of the family because a solvable problem has become
an unsolvable one, owing to the unskillful methods used by the
family member or members.

One important recommendation is to never attempt to solve a
problem when the other family member is not receptive, ready, or
willing to sit down to discuss the matter. It is also crucial to put the
interests of the family unit as a whole before the personal wishes or
wants of an individual member of the family. There are instances
where a parent will allow one child to have his or her way in order
to avoid the child getting emotional or throwing a tantrum. It may
seem that this action by the parent helps in easing the situation.
However, it only gives rise to the child repeating the same type of
behavior over and over again, even into adulthood. As stated above,
parents need to be steady like a rock in dealing with difficult matters. Putting the entire family's well-being above one member of the
family will create room for getting to the root of the problem. It can
also help each family member to see that everyone's wants, needs,
and happiness are vital to keeping the unit wholesome, fair, and
honest. Conversely, placing the blame on one person can close the
door for resolving problems. This can cause the family to divide into
cliques, which can be very difficult to unite into one healthy, loving
family unit again.

The best and most skillful methods for solving any family problems are through the strength of *love, compassion, acceptance, forgiveness, understanding, heart-to-heart communication, and listening
deeply when others speak.* By not acting like the eggs rolling in a pot
of boiling water, the couple should wait until each other's emotions
settle down. The couple needs to reflect on how their love brought
them together, producing a loving child or children. By perceiving
problems in a more holistic way, they can see that problems arise
and may stay for a while, then dissipate by the force of love and respect.

Even with the best intentions, advice, and intervention, there are family problems that cannot be solved. For example — a husband or wife who keeps cheating on the other, being consistently dishonest or selfish, never acknowledging his or her wrongdoing with a willingness to correct the misdeeds, acting in an extremely violent manner, or being highly abusive or bullying. In such cases, it is for the betterment of all involved to end the relationship. This resolution will help to secure the well-being of the innocent children and the abused spouse. Regardless of the reasons for dissolving the marriage, there is no purpose whatsoever for submitting oneself to this type of abuse. Solve the problem properly if it can be solved. Let go of the problem if it cannot be solved. Do so without anger or other disturbing emotions. A very wise man once said: *If the problem can be solved, then there is no need for being angry, unhappy, or worrying about it since it can be solved. If the problem cannot be solved, then simply being angry, unhappy, or worrying is of no usefulness at all.*

The cornerstone for being a happy and healthy family is for **each** family member to have compassion and honesty for all other members of the family. Honesty keeps the family strong and wholesome. Compassion uplifts the well-being of the family and provides a deep sense of solace in the hearts of each family member. This, in turn, creates a sense of joyfulness in living together as a family. Families come in all types and sizes, with different educational levels, financial resources, and types of housing they live in. Along with these, families also have a wide variety of problems to cope with and try to solve. No one truly wants their family to break up, despite the stresses that can and do come about. Therefore, **before giving up on your precious family**, *lift them up on a pillar of unconditional love and build courage within your heart to deal with your family's problems.* Never allow room in your mind for losing their love and abandoning the welfare of your family members. *These directions refer to each and every family member that is considered to be an adult by age of majority, not only mom and dad.*

Particularly nowadays, it is very common to place the blame for our troubles and unhappiness on the outside world — low wages,

CEO's making enormous sums of money, bad teachers, consumerism, and capitalism. While societies certainly have many problems to ameliorate, none of the reasons listed above can cause us or our families to be unhappy. I've often noticed that some families with less money, fewer possessions, and less influence have happier and more compassionate lives. They truly seem to be able to enjoy "the simple pleasures of life".

It doesn't take much money or possessions to lead a simple, happy life, but it does take the right mindset and effort (for both richer and poorer people):

- Be happy with what you have
- Don't blame others
- Give what you can to the needy
- Don't buy what you don't need
- Study and be a good student
- Do a good job at your work

Remember:

- Good people and successful people can be construction workers, teachers, nurses, plumbers, electricians, cooks, or dishwashers, etc. (There is no need to be a doctor, lawyer, or CEO, etc.)
- Be good, kind, honest, trustworthy, and humble to everyone, not only to your immediate family members.
- Then, you and your family will be happy and secure. Guide your children, even your adult children to do the same.

CHAPTER 10

Happiness and Joy

THE OVERALL AIM and purpose of life are to achieve happiness, but happiness may not be what you think it is. Genuine happiness is closely related to our interactions with other people and the world in which we live. *Happiness* is not a *quantity* of what we have, rather, it is a *moral quality* of life and a *wholesome* quality of mind. That is why genuine happiness cannot be found externally — not with other living beings or material objects. Happiness can only be found within ourselves. It is a birthright for all living beings who have a deep-rooted inherent desire for a life of contentment and fulfillment, with the hope of circumventing pain, suffering, or ill will by others. In order to secure our right to be happy, it is vitally important to respect and protect the rights of others who also want to be happy. For this to be possible, each one of us must strive to do no harm whatsoever to anyone through our thoughts, words, actions, or deeds.

Happiness is a principled characteristic of mind and heart that is infused by living an ethical life. It comprises a reduction of causes and conditions (actions and circumstances) that can lead to pain and suffering and embraces the cultivation of causes and conditions that can lead to joy and happiness. Well-paying jobs, money in the bank, material possessions, luxurious homes, expensive cars, and a high social status may be desirable to some people. However, these are most assuredly not the real source of joy and happiness. Happiness cannot be determined by a good job, wealth, possessions, and social status; rather, it is formed by the virtuous qualities of mind and heart.

With this in mind, we can also state that happiness has something to do with contentment. Contentment is a refined quality of mind that eliminates the feeling of unhappiness due to wanting or craving more, bigger, better, and newer things than ever before. We feel contentment when we have everything we want or perceive to need. We humans, especially in this age of consumerism, constantly seem to desire more possessions, and are therefore dissatisfied much of the time. Without being aware of this feeling of unhappiness, or the reason for our discontentment, we keep chasing after more and more worldly goods, leaving us feeling frustrated and exhausted. In these pursuits, we fail to focus on our quality of life. By understanding that seeking quality of life is far better than searching for happiness through acquiring more material possessions, we will become much happier and more peaceful. Our quality of life should therefore be our primary focus. We can then add some additional accoutrements as long as we stay focused on the quality of our lives. In this way, we can find a sense of true happiness.

A great sage once said: *Happiness cannot be found anywhere in external material things and objects. It can only be found within the cessation or reduction of the causes of unhappiness.* Similarly, the Tibetan phrase *Chog-Shey* means contentment or feeling deeply satisfied. It is a state of mind that is profoundly happy with who we are, what we have, and where we live, without drawing comparisons to anyone or anything. To explain this in plain, succinct terms: one soup bowl is enough for one person to eat soup. If that one person has two soup bowls at the same time for eating soup, it is needless and functionless. One soup bowl would simply rest on the table without having any need or function. So, logically we should be satisfied with having one soup bowl to meet our needs. Why would we want two soup bowls? Why would we be unhappy if we didn't have two soup bowls? The lesson is that living happily with a sense of contentment means not desiring or craving what we do not need.

Once we find true happiness, we will develop a feeling of joy, which is an extension of happiness. The feeling of joy gives us a sense of openness and expansiveness to our state of being. This joyful feeling can be sustained with inspiration, admiration, and a stabilized state of mind. Joy does not have an immediate connection to feelings of excitement or elation. Instead, it is an internally pervasive feeling of fresh and unblemished wholesomeness. Unlike ordinary pleasures that diminish quickly, joy can be developed, sustained, and remain constant within ourselves.

The true source of happiness and joy lies within each one of us and needs to be cultivated by us individually, and not with external things. The real source of unhappiness also lies within each one of us and needs to be reduced, weakened, and eliminated through our individual efforts. Happiness is not the same as pleasurable feelings at the level of any of our five senses. We may experience pleasurable feelings when we eat ice cream, drink wine, engage in romantic winks, take drugs, or in love making. These forms of pleasure are momentary and simply a temporary relief from what we are undergoing or subjected to. Any feelings of gratification cannot and will not make us truly happy. In fact, these feelings may lead to negative outcomes such as addiction, cravings, blame, disappointment, and frustration, especially if we do not undertake them in moderation. It may seem that material objects do make us feel happy — a new car that doesn't break down, a comfortable mattress that soothes our sore back, or a puppy that wags its tail and cuddles up beside us. These certainly can contribute to our feelings of cheerfulness and delight, but they cannot provide genuine, enduring happiness.

Genuine happiness comprises a loving and compassionate heart, an ethical mind, and a respectful attitude. To cultivate unaffected happiness, we need to emphasize the quality of life rather than the accumulation of material objects that are more than necessary to survive comfortably. We should be willing to seriously consider other people's thoughts and ideas, rather than opposing or rejecting them. This includes being observant by seeing if others feel comfortable discussing their thoughts and ideas with us without having to be worried about being ridiculed or oppressed. Oftentimes, people may control a conversation by not allowing the other person to speak long enough to get their point across — all in an effort to "win" the argument. Overall, we must be open to cooperate with others even if we may disagree with their thinking. This entails being a good listener and taking time to consider other angles to the subject being discussed. One way to learn how to do this is to stop yourself from giving a quick retort and say: *I understand what you are saying. Please let me think about this for a while, and we can talk more about this a bit later.* You may be surprised to learn more than you thought about the subject, and may end up changing your mind or at least understanding that there is more than one opinion or answer to the topic.

~ ~ ~ ~ ~

An ancient adage states: *All ordinary pleasurable feelings are like a temporary relief from itching when we scratch a rash. The more we scratch it, the larger the rash becomes.* Likewise, temporary pleasurable feelings are not happiness. We should not confuse pleasurable feelings with the true sense of happiness. The absence of having a rash in the first place is far better than the temporary relief from scratching the itch over and over again. Not having any desirous attachments is far superior to constantly fulfilling our desires for the sake of temporary relief from cravings. Neither overindulgence nor rejection, but balance and moderation in all aspects of life is the authentic way to find happiness. There can be different levels of what we consider to be happiness. However, true happiness is directly related to the elimination of the causes of suffering. Thus, true happiness can only be realized by permanently eliminating the causes of suffering. Just as the itch is gone because there is no rash to cause the itch, suffering is gone if there is no cause for the suffering to occur. Freedom from the cause provides permanent relief from the suffering.

We may now understand what genuine happiness entails. But we may still believe that pleasures are good and harmless. Why shouldn't we want things that are pleasurable? The problem with pleasure is that the moment we taste it, we begin to savor it. Subsequently, attachment, desire, clinging, and holding onto the pleasure emerges, and an inner urge to repeat the pleasurable experience controls us more and more. Pleasure is a feeling connected with the idea of beauty, or a sensual feeling involving taste, smell, touch, or texture of something that gives direction to wanting to repeat it over and over again. This feeling of pleasure is a deeply contaminated desirous attachment and leads to cravings and addictions. Pleasure traps and controls us with an unrelenting thirst to pursue the desire. We cling to the idea of pleasure and lock ourselves into wanting it through all means and effort. Eventually, the pleasurable feeling increases our desire and urge for pursuing it, which ultimately leads to frustration, disappointment, confusion, and depression. This is because all contaminated pleasures are in fact the true nature of suffering, although they may appear to be gratifying and agreeable in their nature. Their true nature of suffering is revealed through their change over time, as the more we indulge in them, the less pleasurable they become. This is how contaminated pleasures eventually lead to frustration, disappointment, and depression — the dark emotional abyss in which we become dysfunctional and incapable of functioning well and appropriately in our daily undertakings.

The experience of feeling pleasure is like licking honey from a razor blade. Initially, we may feel the sweet tasting pleasure of the honey, but the instant the razor blade cuts our tongue we are left with a sharp pain that completely ends the pleasurable sensation. Most of us do not see or comprehend the problems that arise when we seek pleasures. We need to understand that there cannot be room for happiness as long as we lock ourselves in the "desire room" and keep pursuing pleasures. Yes, we can find some pleasure from external material things, but that makes us immensely rely on those things in order to maintain our pleasurable feelings. Unlike genuine happiness, we cannot sustain those types of pleasurable sensations. They occur impulsively and dissipate momentarily. This is the nature of ordinary pleasures in which we have all been trapped.

~ ~ ~ ~ ~

No matter how hard we try, or how much money we spend, we cannot buy happiness or even borrow it from someone else. Since happiness is not hidden in material things, it can never be found in any of the world's desirable objects. The key to joy and happiness is found within us but we are incessantly occupied by the causes of unhappiness. These are no other than the bad habits and bad qualities of our mind that nourish the latent imprints of our unwholesome actions, deeds, and behaviors. These need to be weakened, reduced, and completely eradicated from our mind stream. The causes of joy and happiness are no other than the good habits and qualities of our mind and heart. These need to be developed, increased, and stabilized within us. This is the only way that we can have happiness within our grasp and achieve the true happiness we yearn for.

Many of us are occasionally or perhaps frequently unhappy, even though we have a loving spouse, well-behaved children, a comfortable home, adequate money, and a good job. Time and again, we see news stories that a famous actor, singer, or businessman committed suicide. We may be shocked by this news, thinking that he or she had everything to live for. But having fame, wealth, a good reputation, or even our personal everyday good life cannot guarantee genuine happiness. We shouldn't be surprised or disappointed that we become unhappy or dejected, as this is not abnormal. However, hidden below the surface of our external persona is pain and suffering that no amount of wealth or material possessions can cure or conquer. What we need to realize is that, although rarely experienced or understood, genuine happiness can be developed and maintained.

There are three rather subtle reasons why we may often feel unhappy; ones that may seem perplexing or not feasible. The first one to consider is: we have accumulated too many possessions, some perhaps quite expensive or for whatever reason we feel a strong attachment to. Because of this, we may feel trapped in emotions such as fear, craving, or nostalgia, which can lead to an unbalanced emotional state. At some level, we may reason that we have enough tea pots or baseball cards. We might ask our self: *Why on earth do I need more of these, and where will I put them — away in a drawer to collect dust?* We may understand that our questions are sound, yet we are somehow drawn to buy more, and also are unwilling to get rid of the ones we already have.

The second cause may be: when we see what others have, we often feel jealous or convince ourselves that we also need these things. Perhaps a friend recently bought a much bigger house with four bedrooms and five bathrooms. Along with this, the house has a three-car garage, an inground swimming pool, and an indoor elevator. We think to ourselves: *Oh, how this would make me happy!* (even though we only have one child, two cars, and no one likes to swim). We become discontented with our little three-bedroomed house, even though we have paid off the mortgage, and justify buying a huge house; burdened with a large mortgage. We fail to see that what we require for our needs should be enough to satisfy us, and a bigger house, or other things, cannot make us happier. In fact, the big mortgage, higher taxes, and needing to buy more furniture can certainly cause stress and worry, leading to great unhappiness.

The third problem is: we are constantly under the control of a non-stop thinking mind, as our mind is powered by strong and intense thoughts and emotions. They can be fierce "competitors" to our rational mind, and can create thoughts and emotions that are violent, passionate, overwhelming, and irresistible. Our thoughts can irritate our mind and our emotions can depress our mind. These thoughts and emotions themselves are under the influence of *misconceptions* of who we are and the *misperceptions* of the world around us.

These reasons seem to be the most common and prevalent problems for creating our unhappiness, regardless of whether we are rich, middle class, or poor, and no matter how many worldly possessions we have already acquired. It seems as though cravings and wishes do not discriminate regarding affluence or the lack of wealth.

Since our mind unquestionably controls us, we need to overcome our negative thoughts and emotions in order to have joy and happiness within our reach. We may immediately wonder: *Can we really free ourselves from being under the control of our mind?* The answer is: *Yes, we certainly can.* One solution is to learn how to meditate, and then practice meditation once or twice a day. By being sincere with our intention and effort, we can make progress in calming our restless mind. Bear in mind that meditation is not a religious teaching and its practice is not a religious exercise. However, meditation is necessary for the development of a higher state of awareness, psychic power, and spiritual realization beyond the limits of thinking, thoughts, emotions, and dualistic conceptual understanding. By practicing meditation, we can move beyond our ordinary limitations, yet can still remain as *who we already are* but not *what we used to be*: unhappy, extremely difficult to please, hostile, or constantly either defensive or offensive in our nature.

Meditation has become quite popular in today's society. But there are several common misconceptions regarding what meditation is and how to undertake the practice. To meditate does not mean to shut your eyes and make your mind go blank — to "zone out". Rather, it means to clear your mind and make it silent without thinking or being occupied with thoughts and emotions. Simply let go of everything in your mind. Even the "let go" itself should go. Then, sit freshly with a clear and silent mind for a period of time, perhaps 5 — 10 minutes to begin with. During this time period, you should not become distracted or sleepy; the mind should simply be still. Consciously sitting still with a clear and silent mind will help to eliminate irritating thoughts and depressing emotions. You will soon discover that a thought-free mind is a happy mind and a mind free of emotions is a clear mind. The practice of meditation takes time and effort to master, just as it takes time and effort to master playing the piano. Over time, you will become more relaxed and interested in your daily meditation practice. Eventually, your clear and silent mind will help to create a sense of joy and peacefulness in your body and mind.

There are several different types or styles of meditation that can be practiced, depending on your ability. However, there is a very simple form of meditation that is suitable for everyone to learn without too much difficulty. It is called "Prana-yama" meditation and is a breathing meditation or breath-related mental exercise. To practice Prana-yama, follow these directions:

- Sit comfortably in an upright position on a cushion or in a chair.
- Feel relaxed and be yourself.
- Put everything aside but be aware of your intention to meditate.
- Gently bring your mind to your nostrils and, without thinking, let your mind feel the physical sensation as the air comes in and goes out.
- Shift your mind's attention to the actual breath and allow your mind to perceive the natural rhythm of the air coming in and going out in its natural and unaltered way.
- Finally, simply stay with the pure awareness of the breath as long as you can by counting and watching as the breath comes in and goes out without altering its natural rhythm.

This completes the Prana-Yama meditation. If you do this meditation once or twice a day you will begin to feel relaxed, peaceful, fresh, energized, and motivated to live well and do good and wholesome things.

We need to remember that everyone experiences emotions that can upset our regular activities or feelings. Therefore, we need to be aware of our emotions and learn to control them instead of expressing or throwing them on to other people, including our dear family members. Expressing or casting our displeasing emotions onto our family members will immediately destroy the peace and comfort in our home, making the atmosphere in the home feel sad and depressed. No family member will feel good or comfortable living in an emotional home environment, leading the entire family to become unhappy, lonely, depressed, and unwilling to help each other. A dedicated meditation practice, used to quiet our mind and help control our emotions, is the best remedy for our problems and the unrivalled solution for building and maintaining a happy family.

Afterword

IN THIS BOOK we have tried to combine a holistic approach patterned on Eastern thinking with practical advice more common in the Western world to help make family life function better and be more secure. While these perspectives may seem very disparate, they can work well together to strengthen family ties. In our modern world, it can be challenging to find the time to focus on all our family's wants and needs. By combining both types of advice, modern families can find more structure and peace in everyday life.

We often hear that we are in the midst of a global crisis — the world is troubled as never before. This is very difficult to judge, but even if it is so, with optimism, aspiration, and good intentions we can help to overcome misunderstandings, bigotry, and hatred, that can lead to so many misfortunes. Starting with our families, we can help make the world a better place for everyone.

Families are the smallest unit of society, and this is where we truly have the ability to make changes that are worthwhile and beneficial. Improvements in family behavior can result in more understanding and harmony in schools, added cooperation in communities and states, and more accord and peace between nations. We should not fail to recognize the strength and power of the family unit, as families are the lifeblood of society. Simply put, happy families lead to happier and more healthy societies.

With Kind Blessings for a Happy Family Life

About the Authors and Artist

Geshe Dakpa Topgyal, a Tibetan Buddhist monk, was born in the Western region of Tibet. He entered Drepung Loseling Monastery at the age of ten and received his geshe degree (Doctorate of Religion and Philosophy) twenty-two years later in 1992. He has lectured throughout the U.S. and Europe, serves as spiritual director of the Charleston Tibetan Society and the South Carolina Dharma Group, and has written numerous books. In addition to his years of experience and expertise, he brings a kind heart and a sense of humor to his teaching that is both disarming and endearing.

Pamela Harrod spent her career working with students from many countries, first teaching French and ESL, and then as Director of International Admissions at The University of North Carolina at Greensboro. She holds an M.S. in Counseling and Educational Development. A world traveler and frequent visitor to Asia, she founded a boutique tour company  and has since been guiding travelers to the Himalayan Kingdom of Bhutan.

Tsering Rabgyal, a fully qualified traditional Tibetan thangka artist, studied thangka painting and other ancient Tibetan art forms for seven years at the Norbulingka Institute in Dharamshala, India. Since then, he has continued to preserve and promote the culture of Tibet by creating commissioned artwork and teaching the ancient, unique Tibetan arts to students. Having immigrated to the United States from India, he now lives in New York City.